HUMAN PERFORMANCE
AND LIMITATIONS
IN AVIATION

Also by R. D. Campbell and available from BSP Professional Books

FLIGHT SAFETY IN GENERAL AVIATION

FLYING TRAINING FOR THE PRIVATE PILOT LICENCE
Instructor Manual

Student Manual Part One

Student Manual Part Two

Multi Engine Rating

Instrument Flying, Radio Navigation and Instrument Approach Procedure

PPL REVISION
1200 Questions and Answers for the Private Pilot

GROUND TRAINING FOR THE PRIVATE PILOT LICENCE
Manual One: Air Legislation, Aviation Law, Flight Rules and Procedure

Manual Two: Air Navigation and Aviation Meteorology

Manual Three: Principles of Flight, Airframes and Aero Engines, Aircraft Airworthiness, Aircraft Instruments

HUMAN
PERFORMANCE
AND LIMITATIONS
IN AVIATION

R. D. Campbell
DFC, AFC, FRAeS, MBAC

and

M. Bagshaw
MB, BCh, MRCS, LRCP, AFOM, DAvMed, MRAeS

OXFORD
BSP PROFESSIONAL BOOKS
LONDON EDINBURGH BOSTON
MELBOURNE PARIS BERLIN VIENNA

Copyright © R.D. Campbell and
M. Bagshaw 1991

BSP Professional Books
A division of Blackwell Scientific
    Publications Ltd
Editorial offices:
Osney Mead, Oxford OX2 0EL
25 John Street, London WC1N 2BL
23 Ainslie Place, Edinburgh EH3 6AJ
3 Cambridge Center, Cambridge
    MA 02142, USA
54 University Street, Carlton,
    Victoria 3053, Australia

First published 1991

Set by DP Photosetting, Aylesbury, Bucks
Printed and bound in Great Britain at
the University Press, Cambridge

DISTRIBUTORS

Marston Book Services Ltd
PO Box 87
Oxford OX2 0DT
(Orders: Tel: 0865 791155
         Fax: 0865 791927
         Telex: 837515)

USA
    Blackwell Scientific Publications, Inc.
    3 Cambridge Center
    Cambridge, MA 02142
    (Orders: Tel: (800) 759 6102)

Canada
    Oxford University Press
    70 Wynford Drive
    Don Mills
    Ontario M3C 1J9
    (Orders: Tel: (416) 441-2941)

Australia
    Blackwell Scientific Publications
    (Australia) Pty Ltd
    54 University Street
    Carlton, Victoria 3053
    (Orders: Tel: (03) 347-0300)

British Library
Cataloguing in Publication Data
Campbell, R. D. (Ronald D.)
    Human performance and limitations.
    1. Medicine. Aviation
    I. Title   II. Bagshaw, M.
    616.980213

ISBN 0-632-02929-3

Contents

Preface   viii

Authors' note   x

Introduction   xi

Part 1   Aeromedical   *1*

1   **Basic Physiology and the Effects of Flight**   3
    'Fit to fly'   3
    Composition of the atmosphere   4

2   **Respiration and Circulation**   8
    Oxygen and the effects of partial pressure   9
    Hypoxia   10
    Cabin pressurisation   13
    High altitude flight   15
    Hyperventilation   17
    Effects of reduced atmospheric pressure   19
    Effects of acceleration   20

The Human Senses

3   **The Eye and Vision in Flight**   22
    Functional anatomy of the eye   22
    Physiology of vision   23
    Visual acuity   24
    Limitations of the visual system   24
    The visual field – scanning techniques   26
    The airspace, flight rules and the operational environment   31
    Radio equipment and air traffic advisory service   31
    Aerodrome traffic zones   31
    Vision defects   32
      Visual illusions   33

4 Hearing **39**
Functional anatomy of the ear 39
Inner ear sensations 40
Effects of altitude change 41
Noise and hearing loss 43
Orientation 44
Motion Sickness 47

5 Flying and Health **51**
Common ailments 52
Drugs, medicines and side effects 54
  Alcohol 54
Donation of blood 61
Fatigue and tiredness 61
The flightcrew medical examination 65

6 Passenger Care **68**
Anxiety 68
Safety briefing 69
In flight 71
Personal hygiene 72

7 Toxic Hazards **73**
Dangerous goods 73
Carbon monoxide 74

8 Incapacitation During Flight **79**
Scuba diving and flying 80

9 First Aid **81**
Procedures following an accident 81
Fractured or broken limbs 83
Severe bleeding 84
Head injuries 85
Severe shock 85
Burns 86
First aid kits 87

Part 2 Basic Aviation Psychology **89**

10 The Human Information Process **91**
Concepts of sensation 93
  Examples of accidents 93
Perception 94
  Expectancy 94
  Habits 96
Cognitive perception 96

Central decision channel 97
    Limitations of mental workload 98
Attention, information sources and stimuli 98
    Verbal communication 100
Memory 101
    Types of memory 101
    Limitations 104
Stress 105
    Causes and effects 105
    Concepts of arousal 106
    Stressors 108
    Stress overload 109
    Anxiety and its relationship to stress 110
    Effects of stress of human performance 111
    Identifying and reducing stress 113

11 Judgement and Decision Making 116
Pilot judgement concepts 117
Types of judgement 119
Knowledge, skill and experience 121
Exercising judgement 122
    Poor judgement 123
    Examples of good and bad judgement 124
Attitude development and risk management 128
    Behavioural aspects 129
    Risk assessment 133
    Risk management 136
Cockpit management and crew co-ordination 142
    Cockpit ergonomics 146

In Conclusion 155

Bibliography 156

Index 158

Preface

For as long as the human being is part of the aviation system, human capabilities and limitations will influence safety. Given the predominant role of human error shown in accident reports it comes as no surprise that the consequences of human deficiencies have figured substantially in accident reports and other publications. International licensing requirements and the design of equipment, training and operational procedures have all been adapted or changed as a result of experience learnt from accidents.

However, change has been both slow and piecemeal, with understanding of human factors differing within the aviation community. The limitations in knowledge of human capabilities, as well as limitations in aviation, have resulted in a rather incoherent and incomplete approach to human factors training.

There are also various approaches to pilot training, with regard to problems resulting from human factors. These range from dedicated training courses in human factors, aimed exclusively at factual knowledge, through to training focussed exclusively on the development of specific skills, such as communications, crew co-ordination and resource management.

The success of such training has been limited because it has not been fully implemented and there has been a lack of both national and international co-ordination. However, recent developments, notably the publication of the eighth edition of ICAO Annex 1, have changed the situation, at least in respect of holders of flightcrew licences. Publication of the new edition of Annex 1 confirms a growing international consensus that training in human factors is essential.

The Annex now contains a new human factors knowledge requirement for each category of flight crew licence holder: 'human performance and limitations relevant to . . . (the licence being issued)'. This requirement has the same status as knowledge of meteorology, navigation, principles of flight, or any other part of the traditional pilot syllabus. It therefore requires appropriate training syllabi and manuals.

Over the years an enormous amount of research has been conducted in psychology, and the books, papers, etc. which have been published would no doubt fill many aircraft hangars. Most people appreciate that the processes of the human mind and their interaction with the body's physiological functions are extremely complex. A number of facts have been established but many theories still abound which have yet to be proven or discarded.

From a practical point of view, this manual can only touch the surface of human behaviour and how it reacts in relation to aviation activities. It deals with the subject at an elementary level and avoids detailed, highly erudite explanations. Nevertheless, it is hoped that the information on the following pages will bring a greater understanding of how our bodies and minds react in a man–machine environment and will create a greater sense of awareness of our personal limitations.

This manual is aimed at the requirements of the private pilot syllabus on the subject of human performance and limitations, but it will also be of value to a holder of any pilot's licence as well as to other personnel involved in aviation. Human performance and limitations concern the human body and its physical elements as well as the mind and its intellectual processes. The training syllabus for pilots divides these into two main headings, Aeromedical and Basic Aviation Psychology. Because these two are interrelated, i.e. the condition of one affects the other, this manual draws the two together under appropriate sub-headings.

Authors' note

This manual was written in a wide variety of places in Europe and North America, ranging from our studies at home to travelling on public transport flights. On too many occasions it was written during irksome periods waiting at airport terminals because of flights delayed by the incapacity of the current airspace structure to cope with today's air travellers.

These frequent delays strained and yet strengthened a personal quality which is vital to all pilots – patience. Above all, the time spent writing, which otherwise could have been wasted, brought home to us the fact that our current airspace system is obsolete in an age when technical progress can put men on the moon or dispatch satellites far out in the universe to give earth dwellers high definition pictures and other information on the atmosphere and terrain. If pilots are to cope with the problems of an outdated airspace system – which cause frustration to pilots and passengers alike – they will need to gain greater knowledge and understanding of their limitations and the physiological and psychological aspects of their role.

We have to admit that we once thought it was the operational system rather than the flightcrew which controlled our destinies; but the more we delve into the subject of human factors the more we realise that the technical system often fails. If we are to achieve the safety standards we all seek, then pilots, air traffic controllers, engineers and others at the operational end of aviation will need to be more efficient to overcome the limitations of the present airspace system.

So the formal inclusion of human performance and limitations, which is aimed at improving human judgement and decision making, will play a vital role in future aviation training activities.

January 1991

Introduction

Many people experienced in aviation safety now firmly believe that further legislation will not improve air safety in civil aviation. They consider the most practical way of achieving improvement to be through increased emphasis on safety education in general, and the wider application of judgement training techniques in particular.

In other words, current philosophy is moving towards the idea that increased safety will not be achieved by introducing more regulations or increasing the number of periodic checks for pilots or air traffic controllers. We are left with the need to influence more strongly the behavioural patterns of pilots, instructors, air traffic controllers, maintenance engineers/mechanics, etc. by introducing educational programmes to reinforce sound operating procedures and the development of better judgement training techniques. This philosophy leads to the inclusion of human performance and limitations as an organised subject in aviation training courses. It is to explain and promote greater appreciation of this subject that this manual has been written.

While there is a surfeit of books covering the development of flying skills in relation to physical actions and the understanding of aviation technical subjects, for many years there has been a dearth of written material concerning the development of good judgement. It would be wrong not to acknowledge the expertise of people who are involved in the study of human factors, or the fact that a number of excellent books have been written on this subject, but it is not always easy to understand the meanings of many of the words used in such books, and sometimes the terminology can only be found in specialised medical dictionaries.

This can become frustrating and is a major deterrent to the person interested in learning to operate an aircraft rather than becoming an expert in psychology or physiology. Also, in some publications on human factors, one is left with the impression that the emphasis is more on what the author wants to say than on what the reader needs to know to perform more efficiently in a particular role. Thus the reader is often left with the thought, 'Well now that I have read it what do I do with it?'.

The aim of this manual is therefore to approach the subject in reasonably plain language and in a way which helps pilots think more about human factors in the environment of the cockpit and how they relate to the operation of an aircraft, with the hope that readers will be able to understand (without resorting to technical dictionaries) how thought processes can be directed towards achieving good judgement.

Flying instructors aim to impart good judgement but it is generally done in an irregular fashion and only when specific situations arise. This is largely because there has been no structured judgement guidance material or specific goals available in writing. Traditional training programmes in the past have tended to focus on physical pilot skills, including procedural and perceptual activity, all of which are used in controlling an aircraft and operating its systems.

Such skills are generally intended to become automatic rather than cognitive, i.e. thinking or intellectual skills, so only a minimum amount of conscious thought is given to the making of decisions. For example, a pilot needs minimum cognition to know that an aircraft with a retractable gear will need to have it lowered prior to landing. The achievement of safety in this case is totally related to memorising a sequence of checks or drills, and the physical act of operating a particular control in the cockpit in a certain way and at a certain time.

So if an aircraft inadvertently lands with its wheels firmly tucked up, it could not be said in isolation that the pilot lacked good judgement. The actual error was simply a failure to complete the necessary drill, or a faulty manipulation of the landing gear switch or lever. But we must not lose sight of the real issue: what was the cause of the lapse or incorrect action? It is here that a lack of good judgement may have entered the picture before the pilot's error.

A review of inadvertent 'wheels up' landings reveals that in most cases the pilots concerned had been distracted and their attention, i.e. thought processes, were diverted from flying the aircraft or carrying out proper procedures. However, many of these distracting circumstances could have been avoided if the pilot had used good judgement at an earlier stage, e.g. by resolving the cause of the distraction before entering the aerodrome traffic zone or by spreading the cockpit workload over a slightly longer period. Therefore on many occasions, if pilots had received better training in human factors and their relationship to good judgement, they would have been better prepared to handle distracting influences, particularly during critical stages of flight.

As a simple analogy, consider the subject of aircraft performance and limitations as necessary knowledge for pilots. All pilots, through training and experience, appreciate the need to understand how an aircraft performs in relation to take-off and landing, but to do so they have to know in reasonable detail how various factors can affect the performance of an aircraft, e.g., the aircraft mass, density altitude, the effect of wind, surface condition and use of flap, all of which can have an appreciable effect. It is a sad indictment of the safety appreciation of some pilots involved in accidents, that they did not consider these factors or applied their effects incorrectly.

In the same way, and for the same reasons, all pilots should have a basic understanding of human performance and limitations and should appreciate that there are, as with aircraft performance, many factors which affect their own performance, e.g. their physical fitness and problems resulting from stress, fatigue, emotion, anxiety, lack of arousal, etc. In the past a lack of knowledge or appreciation of these factors has resulted in accidents, so it makes sense for the subject of human performance to become a mandatory part of any aviation related training.

It is only recently that the importance of the subject has been sufficiently recognised for it to be introduced into pilot training programmes, and it is hoped that this requirement will act as a catalyst for the development of better judgement and decision making, leading ultimately to an improved aviation safety record.

Part 1

Aeromedical

Chapter 1

Basic Physiology and the Effects of Flight

'Fit to fly'

In addition to physical skills, no pilot can be considered competent unless he or she has an adequate knowledge of the various technical subjects required to operate an aircraft safely. These are not necessarily directly linked to the more obvious aspects of piloting like aero engines, instruments, navigation and meteorology. To understand more fully the scope of their chosen profession pilots must understand certain areas which are usually considered to be the concern of the doctor. This requirement is the 'aeromedical consideration'.

For the same reason that an aircraft is required to undergo regular periodic checks, pilots are required to submit themselves to regular medical examinations in order to establish fitness for piloting duties; while it is not necessary to be a super-person in order to fly an aeroplane there are minimum standards laid down in the interests of safety. Broadly speaking these standards cover vision, hearing and general health.

The modern aviation industry's record in providing reliable equipment and aircraft speaks for itself, but it must be appreciated that any machine is only as good as the person who operates it. To ignore this vital fact would be as senseless as failing to carry out a pre-flight inspection of an aircraft, or disregarding the portents of approaching bad weather. In the same way that a pilot has the final responsibility for determining the fitness of the aircraft, he or she also bears the responsibility for assessing his or her own fitness to fly.

The pilot must ensure before every flight that he or she is free from conditions which might affect his or her ability to perform safely and competently. The air is not the natural environment of mankind so every reasonable precaution should be taken to ensure that when we do fly we do so as safely as practicable.

The Civil Aviation Authority requires, before issuing a licence, that a pilot is physically and mentally able to operate an aircraft competently. This is periodically checked to evaluate the pilot's general health and reduce the possibility of a chance impairment which might affect air safety or the validity of the licence. The authorised medical examiner who carries out the examination may or may not be a pilot, but will nevertheless have a thorough understanding of aeromedical requirements and should be consulted whenever it is necessary to establish fitness to fly as a flightcrew member.

Routine medical examinations are necessary to maintain the validity of a pilot's licence and are required at specific intervals depending on the type of licence and the holder's age. Obviously, however, these medical examinations assess fitness only at the time the examination is conducted, and health and fitness could decline at any time. For this reason aviation regulations make pilots responsible for judging their day to day fitness for flight.

These regulations are quite clear: 'If a person knows or has reason to believe that his physical or mental condition renders him temporarily or permanently unfit to act as a member of a flight crew, he must not act in that capacity.' In other words, if you think you are not fit to fly then you must not fly – as a pilot in command or as any other crew member.

Part 1 of this manual is concerned with the aeromedical facts with which pilots need to be familiar if they are to be professionally competent. It is not comprehensive but it covers the important aspects of this fascinating and important technical subject. By studying them you will be improving your ability to assess your personal fitness to fly, as well as gaining knowledge needed to exercise your duty of care to others, in particular your passengers.

Composition of the atmosphere

The surface of the earth is enveloped in a relatively deep layer of air which we know as the atmosphere. This air is composed of a mixture of gases and water vapour. The basic unit of each gas is the molecule, far too small to be seen. These gases of oxygen, nitrogen, argon, carbon dioxide, neon, hydrogen, ozone and others maintain their separate identities and exist side by side.

This large volume of air has considerable weight at the earth's surface and is approximately 15 lb per square inch, or 30 in (760 mm) of mercury. This represents an approximate total weight exerted on the human body of 20 tons or 18,000 kg. At sea level this considerable pressure is not apparent because the pressure inside the human body is equal to that outside. Figure 1.1 shows the relationship between atmospheric pressure and altitude: the higher you go, the lower the pressure becomes.

In the lower layers of the atmosphere the relative proportions of each gas stay fairly constant. The most abundant gases are nitrogen 78% and

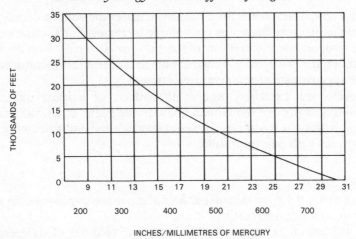

Fig. 1.1

oxygen 21%, with the other gases making up the remaining 1%. Carbon dioxide accounts for only 0.03% yet it is vital to life since plants require it for photosynthesis. In addition, the atmosphere contains solid particles such as sea salt and dust. Because the condensation of moisture is generally thought to occur on these solid particles, they are also important to the development of certain types of weather, such as clouds, mist and fog.

It is essential that a pilot understands both the chemical and physical structure of the atmosphere. Oxygen is required to sustain human life by oxidising the food we eat to produce heat and energy. The physical properties of the atmosphere, i.e. temperature, humidity and density, are also important to the pilot in relation to meteorology as well as human performance.

The physical gas laws

Pilots need to have a basic understanding of the physical gas laws because of their relationship to some of the physiological problems which can be encountered during flight. Since air is a mixture of gases which are compressible it is subject to certain established laws governing reaction to changes in pressure, temperature, volume and density. These laws are: Boyle's law, Charles's law, Dalton's law and Henry's law.

Boyle's law
'Providing the temperature is constant the volume of a gas is inversely proportional to its pressure.'

This means that when the pressure increases the volume decreases and when the pressure decreases the volume increases. Put another way, at a fixed temperature the pressure of the gas varies inversely with its volume. However, the law is strictly correct only at moderate temperatures, being more approximate at temperature extremes.

Boyle's law explains some of the effects of altitude on the gas-containing cavities of the human body during flight: as altitude increases the gas within the middle ear, sinuses, stomach and intestines will expand, sometimes with painful results.

Charles's law
'*The volume of a fixed mass of gas held at a constant pressure varies directly with the absolute temperature.*'

A feature of gas expansion is that equal volumes of different gases expand by the same amount when heated at the same temperature. So provided the pressure remains constant, each degree centigrade rise in temperature will cause the gases to expand by 1/273 of the volume they would occupy at 0°C.

Another way of stating this law is: 'The volume of a fixed mass of a gas at constant pressure is directly proportional to its absolute temperature'. The gas laws of Boyle and Charles can be summarised by the equation:

$$\frac{pv}{T} = \text{a constant}$$

where p = pressure
v = volume
T = absolute temperature

This is known as the gas equation and it applies even when there is a change in all three variables of pressure, volume and temperature.

Dalton's law
'*The total pressure of the gas mixture is equal to the sum of its partial pressures.*'

This law applies to the body's need for oxygen. Since oxygen makes up 21% of the atmosphere at sea level, it follows that only 21% of the air breathed is oxygen. The subject of oxygen and partial pressure is covered in more detail in Chapter 2 under the heading *Oxygen and the effects of partial pressure*.

Henry's law
'*At equilibrium the amount of gas dissolved in a liquid is proportional to the gas pressure.*'

This means that the amount of gas in solution varies directly with the pressure of that gas. This affects pilots in that as altitude is increased and pressure reduces, nitrogen will come out of solution in the body tissues. At high altitude this can cause decompression sickness, often known as 'the bends'. Knowing the danger of this is important to pilots operating at higher altitudes, particularly above 18,000 feet, and even at low altitudes immediately following scuba diving; this aspect is covered in Chapter 8.

Chapter 2

Respiration and Circulation

Respiration is essentially the process by which we liberate energy to maintain life by the oxidation of food. It has three phases, each of which may be affected to some degree by flight:

(1) the exchange of gases between the body and the atmosphere;
(2) the carriage of gases to and from the lungs and the site of oxidation (the tissue cells);
(3) the actual oxidation process in the cells, liberating energy.

Circulation is the term used to describe the passage of blood through the blood vessels. Among other functions it carries oxygen from the lungs to the tissues and returns by-products of metabolism, such as carbon dioxide, from the tissues to the lungs.

Atmospheric air is breathed in through the nose, where it is filtered and warmed, and passes to the lungs via the trachea and appropriate bronchus. Each bronchus ends in a number of bronchioles which in turn end in the alveoli, millions of which form the lung tissue. The alveoli are thin-walled sacs (rather like balloons) which are surrounded by blood capillaries; these are very small thin-walled blood vessels. The thin walls of the alveoli and capillaries allow gases such as oxygen and carbon dioxide to diffuse between atmospheric air in the alveoli and blood within the capillaries.

During respiration, air is drawn into the lungs by the actions of the diaphragm and intercostal muscles; when these muscles relax the process is reversed so that air is breathed out. This cycle occurs between 12 and 15 times a minute at rest and each breath involves about a pint (0.5 litre) of air.

Oxygen from the alveoli combines with haemoglobin in the red cells of the blood within the capillaries, from where it is pumped by the action of the heart to the body tissues. There the oxygen is released by the haemoglobin, and carbon dioxide is taken up by the blood to be returned to the lungs. Most of the carbon dioxide is carried in solution in the blood plasma, although about 5% is carried by haemoglobin.

Unlike food or water, oxygen cannot be stored by the body and so we literally live from breath to breath. However at any one time there is oxygen in transit, in combination with haemoglobin, thus giving an effective reserve of a minute or so. Carbon dioxide can accumulate in the tissues to a limited extent, but a build-up of this waste product stimulates respiration.

Oxygen and the effects of partial pressure

The air surrounding the earth is compressible and has weight. The air at the surface of the earth is supporting the weight of air above it and its molecules will therefore be pressed close together, causing the density of the air to be greatest at the surface. At sea level a healthy person can extract enough oxygen from the air to pursue his normal activities. However, above 8000 feet the effects of lack of oxygen will begin to appear. This is because, although the percentage of oxygen in the atmosphere remains substantially the same up to a very high altitude, the reduction in the pressure of the atmosphere has a significant effect on the partial pressure exerted by the oxygen.

This is a result of Dalton's law: 'The sum of the total gas pressure of the atmosphere is equal to the sum of the individual pressures of the gases contained within it.'

Two examples, one at sea level and the other at 15,000 feet, show the difference in the partial pressure of oxygen.

In the standard atmosphere at sea level the total atmospheric pressure of the combined gases in the atmosphere is 760 mm Hg and the amount of oxygen in this atmosphere is approximately 20%. Therefore 20% of 760 will produce a partial pressure for the oxygen of 152 mm Hg.

As altitude is increased the atmospheric pressure is decreased and at 15,000 feet the total atmospheric pressure is only 430 mm Hg. While the oxygen will remain at 20%, the oxygen partial pressure will have reduced considerably, i.e. 20% of 430 = 86 mm Hg. Thus the amount of oxygen entering the blood becomes substantially less than that required for the body tissues to work efficiently.

Because the efficiency of the gas transfer, e.g. the transfer of oxygen across the membranes of the lungs, depends on the pressure exerted, it can be seen that with an increase of altitude the supply of oxygen to the blood will decrease unless some supplementary oxygen is made available to the pilot.

As a human body ascends it moves into regions of reducing density and pressure, (Fig. 2.1). For example, at 8000 feet the atmospheric pressure is only three quarters of that at sea level and consequently each lungful of air contains only three quarters as many molecules. At 18,000 feet the

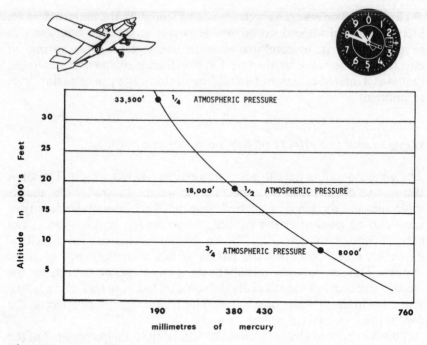

Fig. 2.1 As altitude increases oxygen pressure decreases

atmospheric pressure drops to half and breathing air will give only half the oxygen obtained at sea level.

The rate of oxygen consumption by the body varies with the tissue and its activity. Although the brain is only 2% of the body weight it uses almost one fifth of the total oxygen uptake and is very susceptible to reduction in oxygen partial pressure. Thus the first effects of insufficient oxygen are the impairment of cerebral function.

At 10,000 feet the blood of a person who is exposed to atmospheric air pressure can carry about 90% of the normal oxygen supply received at sea level. The performance of healthy pilots will nevertheless be impaired after a time and they will lose some of their skill and dexterity, becoming slower in working out navigational and similar problems. At 14,000 feet the situation will become more serious leading to a significant lack of judgement and concentration. At 18,000 feet and above pilots will suffer total collapse in a relatively short time.

Hypoxia

This can be defined quite simply as a lack of sufficient oxygen to meet the needs of the body tissues. With an increase in altitude the air pressure decreases and without a supplemental oxygen supply or a pressurised cabin, the amount of oxygen being absorbed through the membranes of the lungs becomes insufficient to support the functions of the various body tissues, including the brain.

Today, in general aviation there are aircraft available capable of flying above 10,000 feet – an altitude above which the effects of hypoxia begin to become serious. Because the human body has no built-in automatic alarm system to let pilots know when they are not getting sufficient oxygen into the blood-stream, and because of the wide variation between individuals, it is not possible to predict the exact altitude at which physical and mental impairment may occur. Another difficulty is that because of the very nature of hypoxia, the pilot becomes the poorest judge of when he or she is suffering from its insidious effects.

Symptoms

A common early symptom of hypoxia is a personality change in which the normal inhibitive forces of common sense tend to be diminished, not unlike the intoxicating effect of alcohol. This progresses to a condition of impaired thinking and judgement, slow reactions, mental and molecular uncoordination, diminished vision and hearing, and impairment of memory.

The symptoms are insidious at first and slow to develop, but progressive and most marked at altitudes above 10,000 feet. However, depending on the pilot's physical condition and tobacco smoking habits the onset of hypoxia can occur at lower altitudes. For example, a pilot who is 'one degree under' or one who is a heavy smoker may suffer from hypoxia at altitudes well below 10,000 feet, and a heavy smoker smoking in flight may feel the effects at about 6000 feet. In all cases night vision is impaired from approximately 5000 feet upwards.

Time of useful consciousness

This refers to the maximum length of time during which a person can carry out some purposeful activity following a sudden reduction in oxygen supply. Fig. 2.2 shows the situation at high altitudes when the pilot or passengers are suddenly deprived of their supplemental oxygen supply, or a sudden failure of the pressurisation system occurs. The figures in this table show that whenever such situations occur the pilot must reduce altitude as quickly as possible.

Altitude Feet	Time of Useful Consciousness
30,000	1 to 2 minutes
28,000	2½ to 3 minutes
25,000	3 to 5 minutes
22,000	5 to 10 minutes

Fig. 2.2

Prevention

No one is immune from hypoxia, so all pilots should anticipate it from observation of the aircraft altimeter rather than relying on the recognition of physical symptoms.

Whenever a pilot anticipates that a flight may go above 10,000 feet he/she should ensure that a supplementary oxygen supply is available. This applies in both pressurised and non-pressurised aircraft. Supplementary oxygen adds pure oxygen to the air being breathed, so compensating for the reduced amount of oxygen at higher altitudes. Supplementary oxygen systems may consist of a portable oxygen container and a mask, or a fixed installation with easily available masks fitted adjacent to the pilot and passenger positions.

Aircraft operating below 22,000 feet often use a type of oxygen system known as 'continuous flow' (Fig. 2.3). This type is usually characterised by a reservoir bag attached to a mask. The oxygen is dispensed from the oxygen storage bottle through a regulating valve to the bag and mask. As the wearer inhales the oxygen from the bag it deflates; as the wearer exhales, some of the unused oxygen is forced back into the bag and mixed with 100% oxygen for the next inhalation. Excess gas is forced out through a cluster of small holes in the nose of the mask; these can also be used to top up inhaled gases with cabin air if the reservoir bag is empty.

To check for oxygen flow, there is usually some form of mechanical flow indicator in the tubing leading to the bag. It is important to check that the oxygen is flowing into the mask because otherwise the wearer will only be inhaling the cabin air.

There are various methods for controlling the rate of flow of oxygen, from manual to fully automatic. In the latter an altitude sensing device is fitted into the system and will change the rate of flow depending on the air pressure. It is extremely important to study the aircraft manual or equipment handbook to establish the correct method of operation of the oxygen equipment in a particular aircraft.

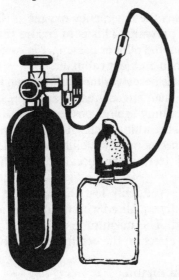

Fig. 2.3

Cabin pressurisation

For prolonged flight above 10,000 feet, the use of supplemental oxygen via a mask is both tiring and inefficient. An alternative method of maintaining adequate partial pressure of oxygen is to pressurise the aircraft cabin to provide a cabin altitude of about 6000 feet, irrespective of aircraft altitude. This may be done by tapping bleed air from the aircraft engine or by using an independent compressor. Today it is not only large, passenger-carrying aircraft which have pressurised cabins; many small and comparatively modest aircraft are capable of maintaining cabin pressure up to high altitudes.

Effects of rapid decompression

Supplementary oxygen is carried in case of the rare event of cabin pressurisation failure.

Because of the risks of decompression sickness (see later in this section), flight should not be continued above 18,000 feet cabin altitude. The supplementary oxygen supply should be adequate to allow descent to this level and continuation of the flight above 10,000 feet. However in many cases the oxygen is provided only as an emergency facility to allow descent to below 10,000 feet, when the oxygen mask may be discarded. (Although hypoxia occurs above 8000 feet, for practical purposes safe flight may continue up to 10,000 feet for short periods of time.)

In many installations the emergency oxygen is delivered to the mask with a small positive pressure. This is to ensure that any leakage at the mask is outward so that the pilot or passenger is sure of breathing oxygen enriched gas rather than ambient cabin air.

Above 40,000 feet it is necessary for 100% oxygen to be delivered under moderate pressure to maintain adequate partial pressure and prevent the onset of hypoxia. Breathing against positive pressure is tiring due to the reversal of the normal breathing cycle. It requires training and should be considered only as an emergency facility to enable a rapid descent to below about 38,000 feet, when pressure breathing should not be necessary.

If cabin pressure is suddenly lost during flight pressure inside the aircraft will be forcefully equalised with the outside air, with the cabin air being rapidly expelled. The magnitude and rate of this decompression, and the physiological effect on the occupants, will be determined by:

- the size of the cabin rupture;
- the altitude of the aircraft;
- the amount of pressure differential;
- the volume of the cabin.

The larger the rupture and the smaller the cabin and the greater the pressure differential between the cabin and the outside air, the more rapid will be the rate of decompression. The term 'explosive decompression' is used to denote an extremely rapid loss of cabin pressure, although this is very rare. However when it does occur a mist will form in the cabin due to the sudden change in temperature.

A sudden equalisation of pressure means a very strong blast of air outwards from the cabin opening. This may cause loose items and even persons to be sucked out. Therefore when flying in pressurised aircraft at high altitudes the occupants should always keep their seat belts fastened when they are seated.

Within the body cavities the free gases will expand and will be expelled where possible. If decompression is relatively slow, the body gases will escape without creating dangerous internal pressures. The middle ear and the sinuses will be ventilated fairly easily because the higher pressure within the cavities forces open the Eustachian tube, which connects the middle ear to the back of the nose, and the sinus orifices.

If the decompression is excessive, gases expanding inside the intestinal tract may cause a certain degree of pain. However because the intestine is normally capable of significant stretching serious injury is unlikely. The same applies to the lungs because the lung gas is usually expelled through the trachea with little resistance.

Following decompression the occupants of an aircraft will be exposed to the risk of decompression sickness and hypoxia. Therefore the flightcrew should make sure that they have oxygen masks available at all times when flying pressurised aircraft.

As mentioned earlier no one is exempt from hypoxia as everyone needs an adequate supply of oxygen. Some pilots may be better able to tolerate an extra few thousand feet of altitude but nobody is far from average and serious trouble awaits the pilot who tries to fly much higher than 10,000 feet, or continues above this altitude for more than a short time, without supplementary oxygen. Pilots who are overweight, out of condition or smoke heavily should limit themselves to a ceiling of 8000 feet unless oxygen is being used or the aircraft has a pressurised cabin.

High altitude flight

The following information is important to pilots who intend to fly aircraft designed for altitudes above 25,000 feet.

Physiological altitude limits

The response to increased altitude varies with the individual. A person who smokes or is in poor health may be affected at a much lower altitude than a person who is young and in good physical condition. Without supplementary oxygen most people will begin to experience a slight reduction in night vision above approximately 5000 feet.

After several hours at an altitude of approximately 10,000 feet a person will begin to display measurable deterioration in mental abilities and physical dexterity. At 18,000 feet the mental deterioriation may result in unconsciousness, with the time of useful consciousness (TUC) being generally about 15 minutes. At 25,000 feet the TUC for most people is 3 to 10 minutes. At altitudes above 25,000 feet the TUC decreases very rapidly, becoming only a few seconds at 40,000 feet.

If a person is breathing 100% oxygen the partial pressure of oxygen in the lungs at 34,000 feet is the same as for a person breathing air at sea level. At 40,000 feet a person breathing 100% oxygen will have the same partial pressure of oxygen in the lungs as a person breathing air at 10,000 feet. Therefore 34,000 feet is the highest altitude at which a person has complete protection from the effects of hypoxia, and 40,000 feet is the highest altitude at which 100% oxygen will provide reasonable protection for the time needed to descend to a safe altitude.

Oxygen systems

There are various oxygen breathing systems available:

Diluter demand
This is a flightcrew oxygen system consisting of a close-fitting mask with a regulator that supplies a flow of oxygen according to cabin altitude. Regulators are usually designed to provide a mix of 0% oxygen and 100% cabin air at cabin altitudes of 8000 feet or less, up to 100% oxygen and 0% cabin air at approximately 34,000 feet. Oxygen is supplied only when the user inhales, reducing the amount of oxygen required.

Pressure demand
This is similar to diluter demand equipment except that oxygen is automatically supplied under slight pressure at cabin altitudes above approximately 10,000 feet, with full pressure breathing above about 38,000 feet.

Pressure demand mask with mask-mounted regulator
This is a pressure demand mask with the regulator attached directly to the mask rather than mounted on the instrument panel or elsewhere within the flight deck. The mask-mounted regulator eliminates the problem of a long hose which must be purged of air before oxygen is delivered to the mask.

Continuous flow oxygen system
This oxygen system is typically provided for passengers. The passenger mask contains a re-breather bag which collects the user's exhaled air, to be re-inhaled. The oxygen in the re-breather bag is replenished by a continuous flow of oxygen regulated as for diluter demand oxygen

equipment (zero flow below 8000 feet, and 100% at approximately 34,000 feet). Because only a portion of the oxygen is consumed during each breath, the air in the re-breather bag remains highly saturated with oxygen and is drawn into the lungs at the beginning of inhalation. If the bag is depleted before the breath is completed, cabin air is used for the remainder of the inhalation.

Both diluter demand and pressure demand oxygen equipment have proved satisfactory for cabin pressure altitudes of 40,000 feet or less when the person using the oxygen equipment is exposed gradually to increased altitudes. However, such equipment does not give protection during rapid decompression to cabin pressure altitudes over 34,000 feet, unless the mask and oxygen are being used prior to the decompression. This is because of the escape of expanding gases from the lungs, and because of delayed oxygenation of the lungs caused by the presence of air in the hose of an oxygen system with panel-mounted regulators. In addition, during rapid decompression an oxygen reversal phenomenon occurs which causes brain de-oxygenation unless a high concentration of oxygen is being breathed prior to decompression. Carbon dioxide diffusion into the lungs, accelerated by rapid decompression, further reduces oxygen partial pressure in the lungs.

Current experimental data demonstrates that moderate to severe decreases in flightcrew performance can be expected under these circumstances. To prevent this, the use of 100% oxygen is recommended for flightcrews operating at aircraft altitudes which may expose them to cabin altitudes exceeding 34,000 feet following a pressurisation failure.

A pressure demand mask with a mask-mounted regulator will provide oxygen at a minimum flow rate of 40%, in accordance with the regulator flow schedule, and will reduce the time needed to displace the carbon dioxide and nitrogen from the lungs. In addition, the regulator can be set to deliver 100% oxygen regardless of altitude.

From this information it can be deduced that at least one flightcrew member should wear and use 100% oxygen during aircraft operational altitudes at which the cabin altitude may exceed 34,000 feet after pressurisation failure.

Hyperventilation

Hyperventilation may be defined as breathing in excess of the metabolic needs of the body. One of the waste products of metabolism is carbon dioxide which is carried away in the bloodstream. The respiratory centre of the brain, which controls the rate of breathing, reacts to the amount of carbon dioxide in the bloodstream. For example, during physical activity

the body cells use more oxygen and therefore more cabon dioxide is produced. This causes the respiratory centre to produce a faster rate of breathing. However, if a faster rate of breathing takes place without an increase in physical exertion, extra oxygen is not taken in so extra carbon dioxide is not produced. The excessive breathing removes carbon dioxide from the bloodstream faster than metabolic production, leading to chemical changes. The result of this is hyperventilation.

Symptoms

The symptoms associated with hyperventilation are:

- dizziness;
- increased sensation of body heat;
- tingling sensations in the fingers and toes;
- increased heart rate;
- nausea and blurred vision.

In extreme cases loss of consciousness can occur but when this happens the breathing rate slows and respiration becomes normal again. Hyperventilation (overbreathing) can be caused by anxiety, stress or excitement, for instance when a pilot suddenly notices that the fuel gauges are reading nearly zero, or during the use of oxygen apparatus if he/she suspects that the supply is not coming through.

The symptoms of hyperventilation are similar to those of hypoxia and it is important for pilots to be aware of how hyperventilation can be caused and the precautions to take to prevent it. Should symptoms occur which cannot be positively identified as either hypoxia or hyperventilation, the following steps should be taken:

- Check the oxygen supply and equipment.
- Put the oxygen regulator to 100% and keep a continuous check on the flow.
- If the condition is hypoxia the symptoms should disappear after three

or four deep breaths of oxygen (recovery from hypoxia is rapid if oxygen is being inhaled).
- If the symptoms persist, consciously slow down the rate of breathing until the symptoms clear and then resume normal breathing rate. Breathing can be slowed down by breathing into a bag or by talking.

Avoidance

A little knowledge is all that is required to avoid the problems of hyperventilation. Since the meaning of the word hyperventilation is excessive ventilation of the lungs, the solution lies in maintaining a normal rate of respiration. If you know that overbreathing can cause hyperventilation and that its effects can be disabling, it is easier to avoid and less alarming if it should occur.

Effects of reduced atmospheric pressure

When climbing to higher altitudes the body is exposed to pressure on its outer surfaces. Because the pressure inside the body is still the same as it was on the ground, the gases inside it begin to expand (Boyle's law). The human body contains a significant amount of gas – largely air and its component gases. Some of these are dissolved in the body fluids, for example nitrogen, oxygen and carbon dioxide. Air also exists as a free gas inside the gastro-intestinal tract, the middle ear and the sinuses, where it expands as altitude is increased.

This phenomenon is known as barotrauma and can cause the occupant of an aircraft some discomfort and even pain. The expanding gases in the body cavities such as the sinuses, behind the ear drum and in the stomach, may lead to headache, ear pain, or a feeling of abdominal fullness. At 8000 feet the gases in the body expand by about 20% compared to ground level. The faster the climb the greater the risk of discomfort or pain. Abdominal gas is present as a result of the digestive process and varies with the individual and the type of food eaten. If one expects to fly at high altitudes in unpressurised aircraft, some diet advice may help to minimise abdominal gas:

Don't
- eat too quickly before a flight;
- eat too much, because swallowed air increases with each bite;
- eat gas forming foods.
Avoid
- large quantities of fluids.

Decompression sickness

In addition to the gases trapped in the body cavities, a considerable volume of gas (primarily nitrogen) exists elsewhere within the body, not in its normal state but in solution. As altitude increases this gas comes out of solution as bubbles and these can produce discomfort or pain around the joints or muscles – a condition known as 'the bends'. Similar bubbles can form in the lung tissue, recognisable by a burning sensation or a stabbing pain in the chest, a cough and some difficulty in breathing – a condition known as 'the chokes'.

Decompression sickness seldom occurs below 25,000 feet and hardly ever below 18,000 feet, but clearly this will vary with the individual and the only possible relief is to descend to lower altitudes.

Finally, bear in mind that gas can be trapped in recently filled teeth, in dental decay or in abscesses of the gum. In these cases the pain can reach levels which could impair pilot ability.

Effects of acceleration

Depending on the rate at which an aircraft's speed or direction is altered, there may be significant physiological effects. When velocity is changed in any way an acceleration will occur, and velocity includes speed and/or direction. The standard unit for measuring acceleration is G, which is defined as the ratio of applied acceleration to gravity (g), i.e.

$$G = \frac{\text{acceleration}}{g}$$

The actual force of 1G for any object is equivalent to the mass (weight) of the object. A person at rest weighing 90 kg is subject to the normal pull of gravity, i.e. 1g, but if acceleration takes place in terms of speed or direction the G is increased, for example in pulling out from a dive the person could experience 2G or more. This is the equivalent of the person suddenly changing his apparent weight to 180 kg.

To sum up accelerative force is measured in Gs or multiples of the force of gravity.

In addition, it may be described by the means by which it is produced, e.g. linear, radial or angular acceleration. The direction of the acceleration in relation to the body axis is described as positive G when pulling out from a dive or conducting a sustained turn; and as negative G when acting in the opposite sense, e.g. a 'push-over' into a dive. The forces experienced with positive G result in the blood and body organs being displaced towards the feet. This tends to force the blood supply away from the head and the heart into the lower parts of the body. If the force is large the heart is unable to pump enough blood upwards against this unusual

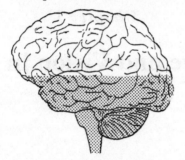

force, and the blood supply to the brain becomes inadequate.

As the effective blood pressure in the brain (and hence the oxygen supply) is reduced, the first symptoms are a progressive loss of vision, a narrowing of the visual field and then, if a large G force continues to be applied, a condition of 'grey-out'. If the G force is sufficiently great the next stage will be a total loss of vision, a black-out, during which hearing and mental function are retained, to be followed by loss of consciousness (G-LOC).

The forces experienced during a rapid 'push-over' can result in the blood and the body organs being displaced towards the head. This negative G condition increases the blood pressure in the head and distends the small blood vessels. The face becomes flushed, with a sensation of fullness in the head and eyes.

Tolerance to G forces is dependent on human physiology and the individual pilot. Factors which decrease G tolerance include hypoxia, heat, hyperventilation and hypoglycaemia (an abnormally low level of glucose in the blood). Alcohol and smoking also reduce G tolerance, as do poor physical fitness and fatigue.

Chapter 3

The Eye and Vision in Flight

Of the five senses vision is used and relied on most. However, it has limitations with which aircrew should be familiar.

In flying, good vision is necessary to avoid obstructions, study the terrain, judge distances, interpret colour signals and instrument indications and charts, and also to perceive depth. Flightcrew must have near perfect vision to operate aircraft with safety. In later years, with ageing, some defects in vision will inevitably occur but many can be corrected with spectacles. Other minor defects may be acceptable.

Flightcrew should have an understanding of certain principles relating to the eye, to obtain the most effective visual results.

Functional anatomy of the eye

The eye is like an organic camera. Both a camera and the eye have a shutter, diaphragm, lens and method of focussing within a container; in the eye this is the eyeball.

The eyeball is moved by surrounding muscles and the lacrimal gland produces fluid (tears) to moisten the cornea. The eyelids act as protective shutters for the eyeball.

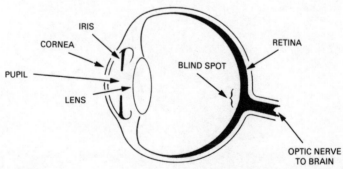

Fig. 3.1

Light passes through the transparent cornea before reaching the lens (Fig. 3.1). The pupil grows larger in conditions of reduced light and smaller when the light increases, thus allowing the correct amount of light to fall on the retina. The lens focusses the light on the retina.

Physiology of vision

The retina has receptors (special cells) which convert light energy into nerve impulses. These impulses pass to other cells in the retina before travelling along the optic nerve to the optic chiasma which is the intersection of the two nerve tracts leading to either side of the brain. The brain has an area known as the visual cortex where information from both eyes is interpreted.

The minute multiple nerve endings in the retina are of two types, differentiated by their construction and function (Fig. 3.2). The small central area of the retina is largely composed of nerve endings called 'cones' which are so numerous that they can detect fine detail. They are needed for maximum visual acuity (a measure of central vision) and also for the discrimination of colour. Cones have the disadvantage of functioning poorly in dim light.

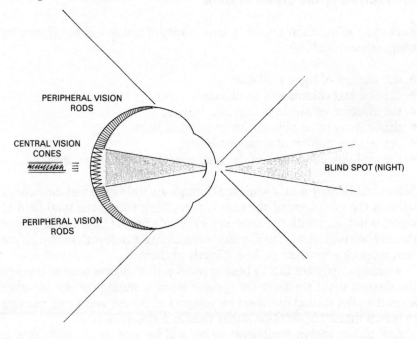

Fig. 3.2

There are other even more numerous nerve endings in the periphery of the retina; these are cylindrical and relatively long, so are called 'rods'. While these have less effect on visual acuity and are not sensitive to colour, they are used in peripheral vision and for seeing in dim light.

Visual acuity

This is the measure of ability to perceive the shape and detail of objects. Flightcrew have to meet minimum standards of visual acuity which are basically established with a standard test card or similar means. The test card must be read from a specific distance and, depending on the smallest letters that the applicant can read, vision is recorded as a fraction. For example, a visual acuity of 6/9 means that the eye, at a distance of 6 m from the letters, can only read the larger letters intended to be read by a person with normal eyesight at 9 m.

Some common defects can be corrected by spectacles so flightcrew applicants can, on occasions, meet the minimum standards even though their eyesight is not perfect.

Limitations of the visual system

Regardless of a person's visual acuity, clarity of vision will be affected by many factors, such as:

- the amount of light available;
- the size and contours of an object;
- the distance an object is from the viewer;
- the contrast of an object with its surroundings;
- the relative motion of a moving object;
- the visibility conditions of the atmosphere, such as dust, mist, etc.

Since visual acuity is best achieved through central vision and diminishes towards the periphery of the retina, everything within the total field of vision is not seen with the same clarity. Just a few degrees either side of the central vision field visual acuity is significantly reduced, so objects are seen most clearly when we look directly at them.

Another important fact to bear in mind is that objects tend to become less distinct when we move the eyes, so when scanning the sky for other aircraft a pilot should use short movements of the eye and head, pausing to search the sky in sections rather than in a sweeping scan.

Any object within peripheral vision will be seen more easily if it is moving. However, when two aircraft are on a collision course the relative bearing between them will remain constant, i.e. they will not move in relation to each other, so peripheral vision is unlikely to be of much help when dangerous occasions such as 'near misses' and 'midairs' arise. Awareness of this should help a pilot develop correct scanning techniques.

Another visual limitation concerns the central vision, as a blind spot occurs where the optic nerve enters the eye. This can be demonstrated by covering the left eye and using the right eye to focus on the aeroplane in Figure 3.3. Move the page slowly closer to the face and at some point the

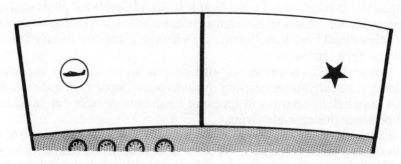

Fig. 3.3

black star on the right will disappear – its image has fallen on the blind spot. Although this does not occur when both eyes are used, the eyes will always be inadequate in that facial features such as the nose prevent the vision from both eyes overlapping.

In normal circumstances looking directly at an object will enable it to be seen more clearly. However, at night or in dim light, this has to be changed as central vision is poor under low illumination. Better results are obtained by looking slightly to one side of objects rather than directly at them. This permits better use of the peripheral vision by using the rods instead of the central cones.

This effect can be demonstrated by counting a group of faint lights in the distance when looking directly at them. Then by looking some 10° to one side it will be possible to see more lights.

A further point to bear in mind is that some people who have perfect day vision may be myopic (near-sighted) at night. Night myopia is little recognised but can present a significant hazard, particularly because of the false confidence instilled from having good vision by day.

A reason for night myopia lies in the differing frequency of colours which prevail by night, and the varying ability of the eye's lens to focus them. Red and orange predominate by day and a lens, whether natural or artificial, which is easily capable of focussing these wavelengths can be found wanting when it tries to focus the more violet colours which prevail at night. In dim conditions the lens has enough elasticity to focus the light from near objects (thus near-sightedness) but cannot focus properly on objects further away.

There is also the insidious effect of age. Most changes in focussing ability are age related and eyesight shortcomings can creep up gradually as the pilot gets older. The problem can be exacerbated in the case of pilots who are already myopic and wear corrective spectacles, as their daytime glasses may be inadequate by night.

As people get older their speed of accommodation also reduces, especially in poor light. In low light it is not advisable for pilots to wear spectacles with photosensitive lenses because when descending into cloud or below cloud from VMC on top, the lenses will take time to adjust to the poorer light conditions.

It is also worth remembering that oxygen supply plays an important part in the ability to see properly. Mild hypoxia impairs the ability to see and to an individual this will appear as a reduction of light – of particular importance during night flying.

Exposure to any degree of carbon monoxide will also impair sight as blood has a much greater affinity with carbon monoxide than oxygen; so in the presence of carbon monoxide the blood will be absorbing less oxygen than is required for good vision to be maintained.

The visual field – scanning techniques

Having reviewed the function of the eye and its limitations, one of the most important applications of this knowledge is when performing a visual scan of the surrounding airspace during flight.

The 'see and avoid' concept can only be employed effectively if a pilot uses correct visual scanning methods. To do this he or she must understand the physiology of the eyes and the psychological aspects of maintaining a good lookout, including an appreciation of the size and speed of other aircraft.

A large aircraft such as a 747 can be seen quite easily when a few hundred metres away, but only when you are looking at it. It is here that we must consider pilot workload and the fact that even when two pilots are employed, there will be moments when no one is looking outside and therein lies the danger. During single pilot operations lookout often becomes what is left of 'look-in' time, so it is essential to distribute cockpit workloads in a sensible manner to allow the maximum lookout and scanning.

The second point is the speed of today's jet aircraft, usually in the order of 500 knots for military aircraft and 250 knots in the lower levels for civil airliners. If we add to this the speeds of closure between two aircraft it takes little calculation to appreciate that an aircraft which is some 10 kilometres away on an opposing heading will take but a few seconds to occupy your parcel of airspace. For example, assuming a closure speed of 600 knots (which equals 1 nm in 6 seconds) and a visibility of 6 nm, from the moment it is humanly possible to spot the other aircraft there will be only 36 seconds before the aircraft meet. This would appear to be plenty of time to take avoiding action, but it is a sad fact of life that pilots seldom spot aircraft at the first moment humanly possible. In fact trials have shown that the time interval between spotting another aircraft and taking avoiding action is more likely to be around 10 seconds. There are many reasons for this, including cockpit workload, the position of the opposing aircraft during the scan period and its contrast with the surrounding environment. Figure 3.4 shows a graphical representation of the changing size of an aircraft closing at 500 knots.

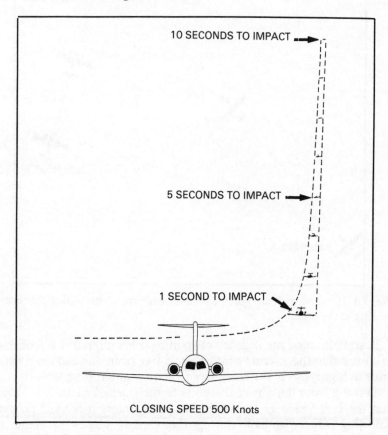

Fig. 3.4 The size of the oncoming aircraft remains relatively small until a few seconds before impact.

It is the relative movement of the two aircraft which is the most important aspect in visibility. Aircraft which move across the visual field will stimulate more of the peripheral nerve endings in the eyes and so are noticed sooner. But an aircraft which has relative movement to the observer is not usually a collision risk. It is when two aircraft are on constant headings, speeds and altitudes and are going to collide that there will be no relative movement between them and they will appear stationary from the cockpits. In this situation one of the most important cues (movement) is missing at a time when the greatest threat is being posed. Figure 3.5 illustrates this constant bearing situation.

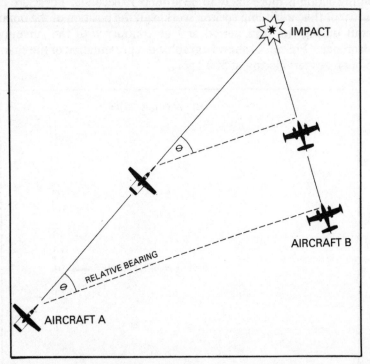

Fig. 3.5 If two aircraft are going to collide, each maintains a constant relative bearing to the other.

Bearing in mind the urgency of spotting other aircraft it is foolish not to ensure that the aircraft windscreen is free from dirt and dead insects prior to flight; this is the best place to start your airborne lookout.

Turning from the physical aspects to the psychological, it is obvious that the best vision in the world is useless unless it is used properly. Knowing where to look during the various phases of flight will considerably improve lookout. This particularly applies when entering an aerodrome traffic zone or flying close to ground based navaids where one expects a greater concentration of traffic. In addition, the information available from radio calls made by other aircraft should be intelligently used to assess when extra vigilance is required and which area(s) to search.

With regard to searching the sky for other aircraft, a further point to consider is 'empty field myopia' which occurs when looking out of the cockpit at an empty sky. Because there is nothing at infinity on which to focus, the eyes focus at a point barely 1 to 2 m away. This is aggravated by the windscreen frame and other parts of the aircraft structure which attract the focussing point in from infinity. As a result the eyes appear to search the surrounding area but are focussed at a very close distance, so aircraft in the surrounding airspace are not spotted. The best cure is to focus on ground objects at frequent intervals, or in poor visibility to focus on the wing tips from time to time.

Pilots must always keep in mind their responsibility for maintaining a good lookout and must arrange their cockpit work cycle so that lookout has a top priority. They should also bear in mind that most 'near miss' incidents and 'midair' accidents occur in conditions of good visibility and by day. A possible psychological reason for this is the tendency to relax more in good weather. The following should be kept in mind at all times during flight.

Visual clearing procedures during aircraft operations

- Pilots should look out in all directions and periodically scan the entire visual field. Remember that the performance capabilities of many aircraft, in both speed and rates of climb and descent, result in high closure rates which limit the time available for detection, decision and evasive action.
- The probability of spotting a collision threat increases with the time spent looking outside, but certain techniques may be used to increase the effectiveness of any scan time. The human eyes tend to focus somewhere, even in a featureless sky, and to be most effective the pilot should shift glances and refocus at intervals. Most pilots do this in the process of scanning the instrument panel, but it is also important to focus outside to 'tune in' the eyes for spotting targets.
- Effective scanning is best achieved with a series of short, regularly-spaced eye movements that bring successive areas of the sky into the central visual field (Fig. 3.6). Each movement should be 10 degrees at the most, and each area should be observed for at least 2 seconds to allow detection. The alternating movement and stopping of the eyes during the scan is known as a saccade/rest cycle. Although horizontal back and forth eye movements seem preferred by most pilots, everyone should develop a scanning pattern that is most comfortable for them

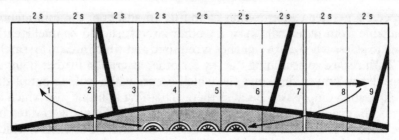

Fig. 3.6

and then stick to it, remembering the airspace above and below the aircraft.

- Peripheral vision can be most useful in spotting collision threats from other aircraft. Each time a scan is stopped and the eyes are refocussed, the peripheral vision takes on more importance because it is through this that movement is detected. Apparent movement is nearly always the first perception of a collision threat and probably the most important, because it is the discovery of a threat that triggers the events leading to evasive action. It is essential to remember, however, that if another aircraft appears to have no relative motion, it is likely to be on a collision course with you. If the other aircraft shows no lateral or vertical motion but is increasing in size, take *immediate* evasive action.

  Visual search at night depends almost entirely on peripheral vision. To see a dim light the pilot should not look straight towards it but should scan the area adjacent to it. Short stops of a few seconds will help detect the light. Bear in mind that lack of brightness and colour contrast in daytime, and conflicting ground lights at night, increase the difficulty of detecting other aircraft.

- Pilots are reminded to move the body as well as the head to see around physical obstructions which are an inevitable part of the cockpit, e.g. door and window posts. Together these can cover a considerable amount of sky and a small head or body movement may uncover an area that is concealing a threat.

- Prior to taxying on to a runway or landing area for take-off, scan the approach areas for possible landing traffic by manoeuvring the aircraft to provide a clear view. This is important even though a taxying or takeoff clearance has been received.

- During climbs and descents in conditions which allow visual detection of other traffic, execute gentle banks left and right to give continuous visual scanning of the airspace ahead, above and below.

- Execute appropriate clearing procedures before entering all turns, climbs, descents, abnormal manoeuvres or aerobatics. When turns are made to search for other aircraft prior to a specific manoeuvre, they should not be limited automatically to a specified number of degrees; the object is to turn sufficiently to make sure that there are no aircraft in the immediate vicinity, and particularly below in the case of altitude loss manoeuvres.

Airspace, flight rules and operational environment

Pilots should be fully aware of the type of airspace in which they intend to operate, so as to comply with the appropriate flight rules. The AIP, NOTAMS, etc., should be carefully studied prior to flight. Up to date aeronautical charts must be carried for the particular route or area. Pilots must be able to interpret the aeronautical legends and symbols depicted on aeronautical charts, and must also develop a working knowledge of the airspace segments and vertical and horizontal boundaries appropriate to their flight.

To reduce the possibility of conflict with other aircraft, pilots must develop a working knowledge of the specific flight rules governing aircraft within the types of airspace they intend to use. They should also be familiar with, and exercise caution in, those operational environments where they may expect to find a high volume of traffic or special types of aircraft operations.

Radio equipment and air traffic advisory services

One of the major factors contributing to dangerous incidents has been the mix of known arriving and departing aircraft with unknown traffic at aerodromes with operating control towers. The known aircraft were in radio contact with some function of the tower (local, approach, or departure control) but the other aircraft were not in two-way radio contact and were unknown to the tower, so traffic advisory information could not be issued to either aircraft.

Although pilots should keep to the necessary communications requirements when operating VFR, they are also urged to take advantage of the air traffic advisory services available to VFR aircraft. When it is not practical to initiate radio contact for traffic information, at least monitor the appropriate frequency, particularly when operating near known arrival/departure routes and instrument approach areas.

Aerodrome traffic zones

Remember that air traffic controller observation of aircraft is often limited by distance, depth perception, aircraft conspicuity and other normal visual acuity problems. Limitations of radar, when available, together with traffic volume, controller workload, unknown traffic, etc. may prevent the controller from providing timely traffic advisory information. Traffic advisories are secondary to the controllers' primary duties which are to separate aircraft and give safety advisories. Therefore the pilot is responsible for seeing and avoiding other traffic. Traffic advisories should be requested and used when available to help see and avoid other traffic, as a supplement to but not a substitute for the pilot's own visual scanning. It is important to remember that advisories provided by air traffic control are not intended to reduce the pilot's obligation to scan properly to see and avoid traffic.

When air traffic control or aerodrome flight information service is available, maintain two-way radio contact with the tower when in the aerodrome traffic zone. Make every effort to see and avoid any aircraft known to be in the area. When entering the traffic zone at an aerodrome which does not have an ATC, AFISO or ground information service be especially vigilant and follow standard procedures.

Vision defects

Binocular vision

As with any occupation using vision, for flying an aircraft two eyes are better than one. Apart from the insurance factor of still being able to see if one eye becomes temporarily restricted by a foreign body or more permanent damage, the use of two eyes (binocular vision) is important in other ways, particularly depth perception.

This is the function of judging distance, both horizontal and vertical. In many situations an individual is unaware of how judgement of distance is achieved, i.e. it is subconscious. Some aspects of depth perception involve only one eye, others require both eyes. In the latter the binocular vision obtained by having two eyes set slightly apart results in the object being viewed from slightly different angles. While this is not so important when viewing objects at long distance, it becomes of greater importance when judging objects close at hand, e.g. during landing.

People who from childhood have only one functioning eye, normally develop the ability to compensate for it. But this is not so easy if an eye is lost at a later age. The loss of an eye is not necessarily a disbarment from holding a pilot's licence but a medical flight test is usually required to determine whether a person with monocular vision is acceptable on safety grounds.

Presbyopia (long sight)

This is a condition which usually develops at 40 to 45 years of age. The lens of the eye begins to harden, so the muscles which pull on the lens to alter its shape and bring images of near objects into focus, have less effect. Reading small print becomes increasingly difficult and books and papers have to be held further away. Spectacles are needed for reading or close work.

Contact lenses are not always suitable for flightcrew and medical advice must be taken. Before a medical certificate can be endorsed approving the wearing of contact lenses, a report must be obtained from an ophthalmologist or contact lens practitioner giving details of the prescription and confirmation that the lenses have been worn constantly and successfully for several hours a day over a period of at least three months. Bifocal contact lenses for the correction of presbyopia are unsuitable for flying and any near vision correction must be made by half spectacles.

If spectacles or contact lenses can correct visual defects a pilot will be able to meet the eyesight requirements for an aircrew medical certificate, though he or she will usually be required to carry a spare pair of spectacles during flight.

Visual illusions

The impulses from the rods and cones of the eye travel along the optic nerve to the brain for interpretation. The eye is very reliable for orientation provided adequate reference points are available. However when flying, one is at a disadvantage when trying to interpret visual cues as objects seen from the air often look quite different from on the ground. So when flying, a person lacks stable visual references.

To someone on the ground the horizon and earthly surroundings are readily visible and only change gradually, if at all. Once in the air, on a clear day a person will observe the earth below, plus other aircraft and, most important, the distant horizon. Equilibrium is easily maintained if the ground and distant horizon can be seen and under these conditions the eyes verify the other senses: proprioceptive sensation (messages sent to the brain from the minute nerve endings in the muscles, tendons etc.) and the vestibular information derived from the inner ear.

If because of weather conditions or darkness the horizon and the ground are lost from view for a time, problems may occur. Even if the horizon remains visible problems can arise during manoeuvres in which the horizon changes position relative to the eyes. Without a visible horizon a pilot may mistakenly choose another line as a reference and fly parallel to a sloping cloud bank for example, instead of the earth's surface.

Many illusions can be experienced in flight. Some can lead to spatial disorientation, others to landing errors. Illusions rank among the most common factors which contribute to accidents, so the following examples will be useful to all pilots.

Auto-kinesis
In the dark a static light will appear to move when stared at for several seconds. The apparent movement will increase if the object is allowed to become the prime focus of attention and it is possible for the pilot to lose control of an aircraft in attempting to align it with the light. To lessen the effects of this visual illusion, shift the gaze so as not to stare at the source of light.

Illusions leading to landing errors
Various surface features and atmospheric conditions can create illusions of incorrect height and distance from the runway threshold. Landing errors from these illusions can be avoided by anticipating them during approaches and making visual inspections of unfamiliar aerodromes or landing strips before landing. The correct use of precision landing aids, VASI and PAPI installations will also assist judgement during the approach and landing.

Ground lighting illusions
Lights along a straight path, such as a road, and even lights on moving vehicles can be mistaken for runway or approach lights. Bright runway and approach lighting systems, especially where few lights illuminate the surrounding terrain, may create the illusion of there being less distance to the runway threshold. A pilot who does not recognise this illusion will tend to fly an incorrect approach path. The pilot overflying terrain which has few lights to provide height cues may make a lower than normal approach.

Atmospheric illusions
Rain on the windscreen can create the illusion of greater height, and atmospheric haze can create the illusion of being further from the runway. The pilot who does not recognise these illusions will probably fly an incorrect approach path. When penetrating mist or fog an illusion of pitching up can occur and can cause the pilot to steepen an approach quite abruptly.

Runway and terrain slope illusion (Fig. 3.7)
An upsloping runway, or terrain, or both can create the illusion that the aircraft is at a higher altitude than it actually is. A pilot who does not recognise this illusion will tend to fly a lower than normal approach. A runway or approach terrain which slopes down can have the opposite effect.

An upsloping runway can create the illusion that the aircraft is higher than it actually is, leading to a lower approach.

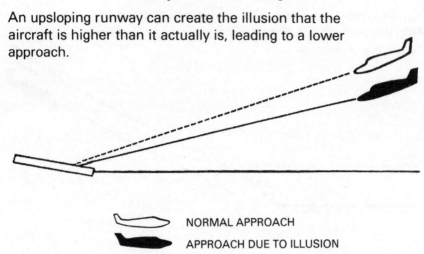

NORMAL APPROACH

APPROACH DUE TO ILLUSION

A downsloping runway can create the illusion that the aircraft is lower than it actually is, leading to a higher approach.

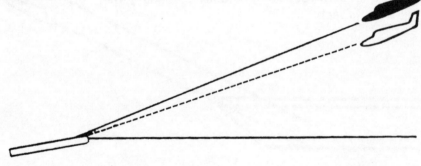

Fig. 3.7

Runway width illusion (Fig. 3.8)
When approaching a runway that is narrower than usual, it may appear that the aircraft is higher than it actually is. If this is not appreciated, the pilot will tend to fly a lower approach than normal. Runways significantly wider than those normally used will give a pilot the impression of being lower than normal, and will increase the risk of levelling out high and causing a hard landing or even an overshoot of the runway.

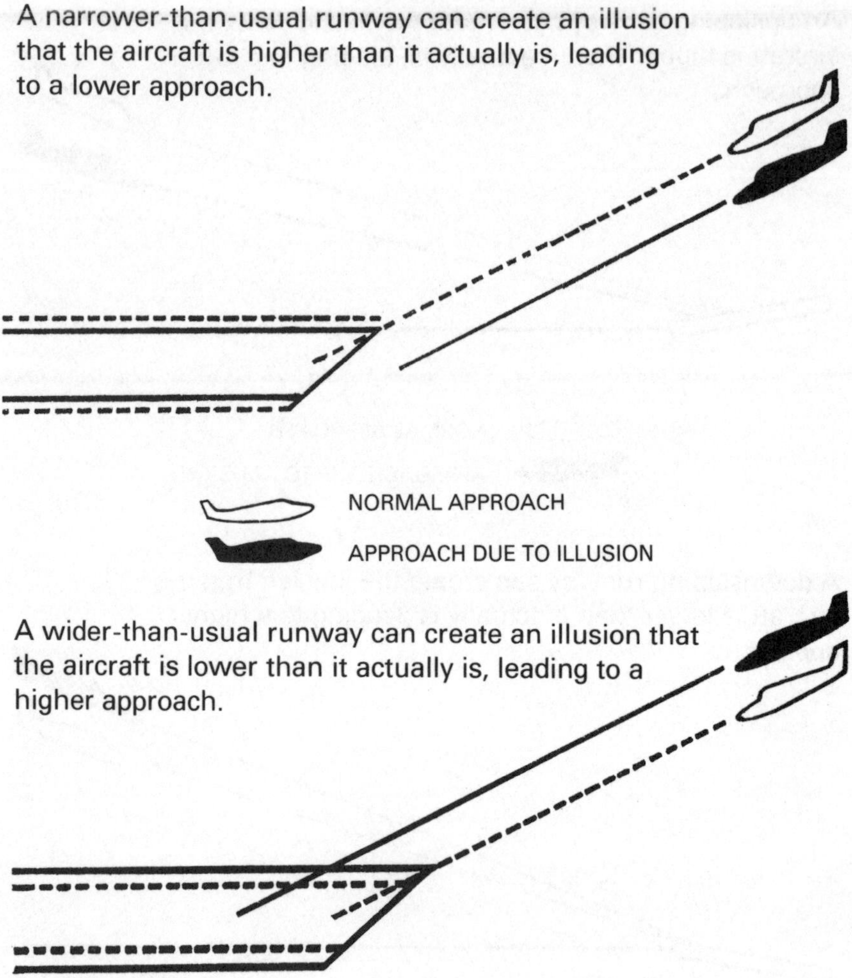

A narrower-than-usual runway can create an illusion
that the aircraft is higher than it actually is, leading
to a lower approach.

NORMAL APPROACH

APPROACH DUE TO ILLUSION

A wider-than-usual runway can create an illusion that
the aircraft is lower than it actually is, leading to a
higher approach.

Fig. 3.8

Featureless terrain

An absence of visible ground features, such as when approaching to land
over water, darkened areas or terrain made featureless by snow, can create
the illusion that the aircraft is at a higher altitude than it actually is,
leading the pilot to fly a lower than normal approach.

When landing at night at an aerodrome with no surrounding lights,
pilots face what has become known as the 'black hole'. Robbed of their
normal visual cues and presented with an unfamiliar set of indicators
about their position in space, pilots have demonstrated a tendency to

make excessively low approaches, some low enough to end up short of the runway. Research shows that this is the result of misinterpreting the slant of the runway relative to the straight ahead direction. Such a misinterpretation may result from the absence of visual information on either side of the runway. This type of information is normally used by pilots when constructing their view of reality. When deprived of normal cues the brain starts searching for something, and what it finds is the runway edge lights from which it calculates where it thinks the runway is. Unfortunately, using the narrower width of the runway edge lights can lead to errors in the approach angle, which may leave the pilot low, slow and running out of options.

The effect of rain
Apart from reducing forward visibility, three other specific effects occur when rain is on the windscreen:

- Objects are obscured by an overall blurring effect.
- A prismatic effect is caused by light being refracted. This can cause an apparent downward displacement of objects when viewed through a rain covered windscreen, thus making the runway seem lower during an approach to landing.
- There is a diffusion of light, or 'halo effect'. This can make lights seem further apart and less intense, and so further away than their actual distance.

Remember that visual illusions seem very real, and that they occur in pilots of every level of experience and skill. The ability to recognise that your brain can play tricks on you in this manner is your only source of protection.

Defective colour vision
Difficulty in distinguishing between colours, particularly red and green, is an inherited defect and is permanent. It is much more common in males and affects about 8% of all men as opposed to about 0.4% of women.

The discrimination of colour is entirely dependent on the cones of central vision. Individuals who have below average ability to differentiate colour are often said to be colour blind, but a better term is 'colour defective' as total colour blindness is rare.

The most common type of defect is the inability to distinguish between red and green – they are seen as a neutral shade. In partial red–green blindness both colours are seen as a darker shade. Good colour vision is essential for flightcrew because of coloured navigation lights on aircraft and lights at aerodromes and on ground obstructions. There is also the need to interpret coloured maps, recognise ground features and coloured emergency flares and light signals, as well as colour coded instruments in the cockpit.

Most people have no difficulty living with colour defective vision and it does not prevent them from holding a driving licence; indeed, no link has yet been established between colour defective vision and road accidents. It has been suggested that colour vision is now less important for aircrew, as light signals are used less frequently for air traffic control. However, with the development of electronic instruments and flight system displays on flight decks, the ability to differentiate between subtle colour shades has become, if anything, more important, and safe colour vision is likely to remain a medical requirement for the issue of a licence.

Chapter 4

Hearing

Functional anatomy of the ear

The ear consists of three parts: the outer ear, the middle ear and the inner ear (Fig. 4.1). The outer ear is composed of the ear flap and the ear canal. The middle ear contains the ear drum, the auditory ossicles (sound conducting bones) and the Eustachian tube. The inner tube contains the cochlea (organ of hearing) and the balance mechanism.

The ear flap collects sounds and directs them along the ear canal to the ear drum. Sounds, which are small fluctuations in air pressure, cause the drum to vibrate. For the drum to be sensitive to sound, the air in the

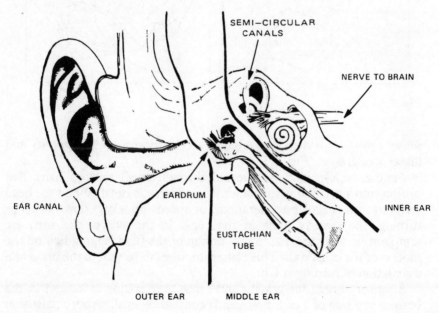

Fig. 4.1

middle ear must be at the same pressure as the air in the outer ear and this pressure is equalised by the Eustachian tube which connects the ear with the back of the throat. When climbing or descending, a 'popping' sensation is usually felt and is the result of uneven pressures being equalised between the outer and middle ear.

Besides being the organ of hearing, the ear also contains the organ of balance. This lies within the inner ear and consists of three semi-circular canals inter-connected and containing a fluid. When the head moves, the relative movement between the fluid and the canal displaces the receptor which sends a signal to the brain via the auditory nerve.

Inner ear sensations

The semi-circular canals form a motion sensing system and are arranged approximately at right angles to each other, in the roll, pitch and yaw axis. The system is shaped as shown in Figure 4.2 and contains fluid and the

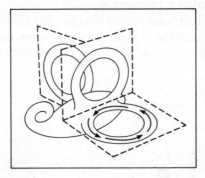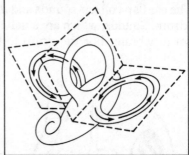

Fig. 4.2

sensory organs for detecting angular acceleration as well as gravity and linear acceleration (Fig. 4.3).

Angular acceleration is detected through small sensory hairs that project into a gelatinous substance located in each canal. When the head starts to turn (angular acceleration), or speeds up, slows down or stops turning, the sensory hairs in the canal in the axis of the turn are temporarily deflected due to the motion of the fluid lagging behind the motion of the canal wall. This causes impulses to be sent to the brain and a sensation of turning is felt.

A sensory organ for gravity and linear acceleration is located in the bottom and side of a common sac. It consists of small sensory hairs that project upward into a gelatinous substance containing chalk-like crystals.

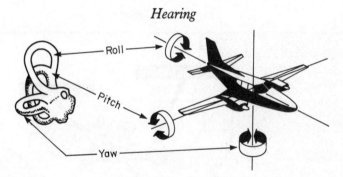

Fig. 4.3

The weight borne by these sensory hairs changes with every head movement up, down, left, right, forward and backward, thus causing the sensation of tilting the head or body.

Evolutionary development has equipped mankind to use these sensory messages when on the surface of the earth. However, once a person becomes airborne misleading messages can be received causing a state of disorientation. Equilibrium, its relationship to the basic sensory perceptions and the causes of disorientation are covered later in this chapter.

Effects of altitude change

Consistent with Boyle's Law, the air in the cavity of the middle ear expands and contracts with changes in atmospheric pressure. During a change in altitude, if the pressure in the ear is not readily equalised with the outside pressure, the drum is distended and inflammation, with pain and temporary deafness, can occur. This condition has been given the name 'aerotitis' and is common to those who fly. To appreciate how aerotitis occurs an understanding is needed of how the Eustachian tube functions (Fig. 4.4). This tube leads from the middle ear to the back of the throat, so the middle ear communicates with the outside air and in normal conditions any difference between the middle ear and the outside atmosphere is equalised. The tube remains in a collapsed state except when it is briefly opened by swallowing or yawning.

When the air in the middle ear expands, as for example during a climb, a small bubble of air is forced out through the Eustachian tube at frequent intervals. Normally no difficulty is experienced during a climb to higher altitudes because pressure equalisation occurs automatically. However during a descent the situation is reversed. As the surrounding air pressure increases, the middle ear, which has accommodated to the reduced pressure at altitude, is at a lower pressure than the external ear canal. Consequently, the increasing pressure of the outside air forces the

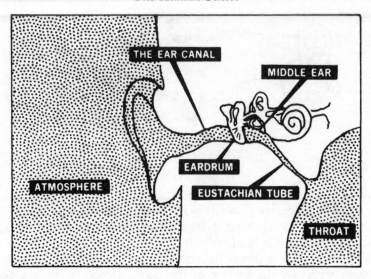

Fig. 4.4

eardrum to bulge inward. This is much more difficult to relieve because air must now go back up the Eustachian tube to equalise the pressure between the inner ear and the outside atmosphere. The lower pressure in the Eustachian tube tends to collapse the tube rather than inflate it. This produces a sense of fullness, discomfort and even pain and temporary deafness.

Normally, ventilation of the middle ear during a descent can be achieved by frequent swallowing or yawning, producing a contraction of the small throat muscles which briefly open the Eustachian tube. When swallowing or yawning has no effect, keep the mouth closed, pinch the nostrils shut and blow slowly and gently to build up pressure in the mouth and nose.

The important point is to ventilate the ears at frequent intervals during any descent, and if it becomes difficult the rate of descent should be decreased or even stopped at intervals to allow more time for the pressure to equalise.

Flying while suffering from a cold or other upper respiratory infection is inadvisable because the tissue around the nasal end of the Eustachian tube will probably be swollen. This can cause the small orifice of the tube to be restricted or even closed, with resulting difficulty in equalising the pressure. If the pressure cannot be equalised there will be a risk of the eardrum becoming perforated, needing medical treatment.

Noise and hearing loss

Noise can be an unpleasant sound produced by the acoustic waves of scattered frequencies. The principal effects of noise in the cockpit are interference with radio and voice communication, additional fatigue, and hearing deterioration. Non-pressurised propeller type aircraft cause more cockpit noise than jet aircraft.

Hearing starts at the outer ear which collects sound waves and conducts them to the middle ear, causing the eardrum to vibrate. This sets up motion in the small bones of the middle ear through which vibrations are passed on to the cochlea. These stimuli are then transmitted via the auditory nerve to the brain where the vibrations are perceived as sound. There are two measurable components of sound and these are 'loudness' (intensity) and 'tone' (pitch). Thus two different sounds can have the same intensity but a different pitch.

Individuals vary so it is not possible to specify the maximum sound levels or duration that the ear will tolerate without permanent hearing impairment. Limits are, however, specified for industrial personnel. It is known that hearing declines with age (presbycusis) and that individual factors play a role in determining whether a person finds a noise level unacceptable. What is also fairly obvious is that loud noise, apart from being unpleasant, is distracting and makes concentration on operating an aircraft difficult.

Hearing loss is normally slow, insidious and progressive. Each unprotected exposure to loud noise or high pitched sounds causes damage until the threshold is reached and hearing impairment becomes apparent. Therefore it makes sense to avoid, where possible, excessive noise in and out of the cockpit. Noise-attenuating headphones are a good method of protecting the ears, but some pilots have the volume control of their radios set at a higher level than necessary, which offsets some of the protection.

The use of earplugs during flight is also a good protection but the wearer should take particular note of the manufacturer's instructions as in most cases it is not just a simple matter of popping them in the ears. A further point to bear in mind is that when earplugs are tight fitting it may be more difficult to equalise the pressure between the middle ear and the outside atmosphere when descending. Nevertheless, because good hearing is vital to flightcrew, earplugs (in non-radio aircraft) or headsets should be used whenever possible to keep the hearing in good shape.

Finally, bear in mind that the main concern about noise is its long term effect on hearing. Short term impairment after a flight is common and usually benign; it is the gradual deterioration of hearing that flightcrew must guard against.

Orientation

The body's sensory organs – the eyes, the vestibular organs of the inner ear and the nerve endings in the skin, muscles and joints – pass messages to the brain. The brain interprets these messages and decides whether we are standing, sitting, upright, leaning to the left or right, backward or forward, the right way up, upside down etc.

When the body is functioning in its natural environment, on the surface of the earth, it is usually able to determine its attitude easily. However, flying is an unnatural environment for human beings and the brain can receive conflicting messages from individual sensory organs, leading to disorientation.

Sensory illusions and spatial disorientation

These mainly occur when the sensory organs send conflicting messages to the brain, leading to a state of confusion. This causes spatial disorientation which is a false perception of the orientation of the aircraft, with respect to spatial references such as flight path and height.

Complex and interactive forces (which cannot be distinguished from the force of gravity) can create specific illusions unless corrected by the powerful sensation of sight. So when external visual reference is restricted, e.g. flying in cloud or conditions of poor visibility, conflicting sensory information cannot be corrected unless a pilot has been trained to use and firmly believe in the information given by the flight instruments.

In the absence of reliable visual information, the motion and position sensing systems tend to take over and at times this can give very misleading information to the brain.

Visual illusions were covered in the previous chapter, and some can create disorientation. Further illusions which can result from misleading indications of the motion and position sensing systems are outlined below.

Illusion of level flight

In straight and level flight, the fluid in the semi-circular canals of the ear is stationary and the hair detectors are not deflected. Any movement of the head, as a result of aircraft roll or pitch, will cause a reaction in the appropriate canal and a signal is sent to the brain so that it can detect the direction of the movement. This signal is the result of the hairs being deflected by the relative movement of the fluid, but continuing the motion at a steady rate will allow the fluid to catch up with the aircraft and the hairs will revert to their original upright position.

This gives a false indication to the brain that the aircraft is once again flying straight and level. If the attitude cannot be confirmed visually the pilot will think the aircraft is level, but as the aircraft is turning there will be a tendency for the nose to lower, resulting in increased airspeed. If the pilot now eases back on the control column to counteract this increase, the turn will tend to steepen and the aircraft will descend. The result of this is fairly obvious: the pilot will increase the back pressure on the control column causing an even steeper angle of bank, and the aircraft will soon be in a spiral dive.

Illusion of turning in the opposite direction

Another illusion can occur when recovering to level flight after a turn. During the turn the fluid in the canal has stopped moving as a steady state is achieved. As the wings are levelled, the rolling motion stimulates the appropriate semi-circular canal and the fluid continues to flow after the canal has come to rest. This leads to a sensation of turning in the opposite direction. The pilot will therefore tend to bank the aircraft away from the imaginary turn.

Illusion of turning in a different axis

An abrupt head movement during a prolonged constant rate turn may set the fluid in more than one semi-circular canal in motion, causing the strong sensation of turning or accelerating in a different axis. In attempting to offset this the pilot may become seriously disoriented, leading to difficulty in maintaining a safe aircraft attitude.

Illusion of tumbling backwards

An abrupt change from climbing to level flight can cause excessive stimulation of the sensory organs for gravity and linear acceleration, thus creating the illusion of tumbling backwards. To correct this the pilot may push the control column forward to lower the nose, and intensify the original false impression.

Illusion of climbing

In a correctly balanced turn the acceleration tends to push the body firmly into the seat, as when an aircraft is being pulled into a climb or pulled out from a dive. If no visual reference is available this force may be interpreted as entering a climb and the pilot may react by moving the control column forward.

Illusion of diving

The positive G force of a banked turn will be reduced when recovering to level flight. This reduction may be interpreted by the pilot as entering a dive and may cause him or her to apply back pressure to the control column and produce a significant reduction in airspeed.

Disorientation when rotating

Severe disorientation and vertigo can occur if the aircraft is rolling and the pilot moves his or her head out of the plane of rotation; two sets of semi-circular canals are stimulated. A harsh pull out of a dive while rolling will produce the same effect, typically when pulling out from a dive following a spin, before the rotation of the canal fluid has ceased.

If rotary motion occurs for a short period, e.g. a spin, when it stops there will be a sensation of rotation in the opposite direction, due to the continuing rotation of the fluid. With poor visual cues, it is possible for the pilot, in correcting for this false illusion, to put the aircraft into a spin in the opposite direction.

Vertigo

This is the ultimate sensation of spatial disorientation, in which the individual or his surroundings appear to whirl dizzily. It may be accompanied by nausea or vomiting and is a result of a disturbance in the vestibular apparatus. This can be due to disease, in which case it is long term, but when it occurs in flight it is usually temporary, lasting a few seconds.

Prevention of disorientation

Disorientation can never be completely avoided but there are ways of minimising its effect. One must appreciate that illusions stem from normal perceptions during flight, and they can and must be ignored or suppressed by believing the aircraft instruments rather than physical sensations.

Experience and continuous practice in instrument flying are the best ways of discounting or overcoming false sensations. Precautions to take include:

- Never continue flying in deteriorating weather conditions unless suitably qualified in instrument flying.
- Never continue into dusk or darkness unless competent in the use of the flight instruments.
- Avoid sudden head movements in flight, particularly when manoeuvring.

- Ensure that when outside visual references are used they are reliable, fixed points on the earth's surface.
- Do not fly with a cold or any other illness.
- Do not drink alcohol within 12 hours of take-off as its after-effects make the semi-circular canals more sensitive.
- Do not fly when tired or 'one degree under'.
- Keep practising instrument flying.

Although a major cause of spatial disorientation is lack of visual cues, even the eyes can be deceived in certain circumstances, particularly when visibility is partly restricted. Therefore added care must be taken when a good horizon or clear ground features are not visible. Patchy fog, mist, smoke, haze, dust or ice particles can all contribute to illusion, and flight between cloud layers or banks of cloud, over water or at night can all create conditions for disorientation.

Lights flashing from four to twenty times a minute or flashing very rapidly can produce unpleasant and dangerous reactions in some individuals. These may include nausea and even convulsions, or epilepsy.

In single engined aircraft when heading directly towards or away from the sun, 'vertigo' can be caused by the propeller cutting the sunlight and giving a flickering or stroboscopic effect. This can be avoided by not staring directly through the propeller disc and by changing the RPM. When in or close to clouds, rotating beacons or strobe lights may also create visual illusions and may have to be switched off.

Motion sickness

Motion sickness is a normal human response to unfamiliar motion and affects different individuals in different ways. Some people are totally unaffected by motion, whereas others suffer severe nausea and vomiting at the mere mention of the words cross-channel ferry or Cessna 150! Most people lie somewhere between the two.

Cause

Sickness is a fairly common problem in early flying training and in passengers unfamiliar with flight in light aeroplanes. The cause is complex and not fully understood, but there is no doubt that the vestibular apparatus in the inner ear plays an essential role.

Information on orientation and motion within the spatial environment is provided by the eyes, inner ear receptors and nerve endings in the muscles and joints. As we grow up we learn to associate specific patterns of sensory information with motion in relation to what we are seeing.

Motion in flight, at sea, in a car or in a space shuttle generates patterns of sensory input which conflict with those patterns based on terrestial experience. The brain is upset by this conflict, and motion sickness results. The strength of the signals generated by the vestibular system appears stronger in some people than in others, i.e. some have more sensitive vestibular systems.

Anxiety and hyperventilation also play an important part in the development of motion sickness. When a person is anxious and tense the whole nervous system becomes extra sensitive, and if the vestibular system is already sensitive the anxiety can take it above the critical level. Hyperventilation acts in a similar way, by raising the individual's arousal level (or maybe the increased arousal leads to the hyperventilation). This again increases the sensitivity of the vestibular system, making motion sickness more likely in a susceptible individual.

The after-effects of alcohol may play an important role in the development of motion sickness. It is well accepted that aircrew should not fly within at least 12 hours of drinking alcohol. However, it is often not realised that the effects of even small quantities of alcohol may be detected in the vestibular system for several *days* afterwards.

Alcohol diffuses from the bloodstream into the fluid (endolymph) in the semi-circular canals. Because it is less dense than water the alcohol does not become evenly distributed within the endolymph, but creates a light spot which causes the fluid to move within the semi-circular canal as if the head was turning. This increases the sensitivity of the canal, leading to the well-known sensation of the head spinning. However, when the head-spinning sensation ceases with the removal of the alcohol from the bloodstream, the increased sensitivity of the canals remains for some time.

Symptoms and signs

The earliest symptom of motion sickness is usually unease in the stomach. Hyperventilation is common. The victim's face is usually pale and he or she begins to sweat. This is followed by increased salivation, a feeling of body warmth, light-headedness and, occasionally, depression and apathy. By this stage vomiting is usually not far away, although some people remain severely nauseated for long periods and do not obtain the transitory relief of vomiting.

Many people find motion sickness severely debilitating and have great difficulty functioning efficiently and safely. Other people find that once they have vomited they feel well again and can carry on with the task in hand with no problems.

Prevention

The human body has a remarkable ability to adapt to changes in environment or to new sensations. With continued exposure to a provocative environment, such as flying in a light aeroplane, it seems that the new sensory patterns become accepted as the norm by the brain and motion sickness happens less easily. However, this requires regular exposure to the environment, which explains why some experienced aircrew suffer from nausea or sickness on their first flight after a break.

To help prevent motion sickness keep stimulation of the semi-circular canals to a minimum; this means that head movements should be limited, within the requirements of maintaining adequate lookout. If an individual is known to be susceptible to motion sickness, this advice should be followed *before* the onset of symptoms. The same applies to passengers unused to flying.

Vision plays a strong part and it is therefore good practice to fix the gaze on a stable distant horizon. If there is no horizon, e.g. in cloud, it often helps to rest the head on the back of the seat and keep the eyes closed (assuming someone else is flying the aeroplane!).

Bending the head forward to read induces motion sickness in a susceptible individual and it may help to bring maps and checklists up level with the coaming. This has the added bonus of improving lookout. Passengers should be discouraged from reading in flight, and it helps to keep them occupied by drawing their attention outside, to things at a distance. Be on your guard for impending air sickness when the passenger goes quiet, looks pale and begins to sweat and hyperventilate.

There is much conflicting advice on whether one should eat before a flight. In fact, it makes little difference. The origin of motion sickness is the vestibular system, not the stomach, so the best advice is to eat as normal and maintain a good blood sugar level. Similarly, smells and heat are not causes. However, if one is starting to feel unwell, unpleasant smells and a stuffy atmosphere become more intrusive and contribute to the feeling of malaise.

There are many drugs available to counteract motion sickness. Some are only available on prescription, but others can be bought over the counter. All these drugs, however, have side effects which can affect flying performance, including drowsiness, increased reaction time, poor muscular co-ordination and a reduced rate of information processing. Different people react in different ways, but the drugs affect everybody to some extent. They are suitable for use by passengers and in certain circumstances may be used by student pilots when flying dual with an instructor. But *these drugs must not be taken by pilots flying solo or as captain.*

Of the drugs available the most effective is hyoscine (sold as Kwells). Cinnarizine (sold as Stugeron) is effective for longer but must be taken at least 30 minutes before getting airborne. Both these drugs have the side effects mentioned above.

Other preventive measures which have been suggested include wrist bands which apply pressure at the acupuncture point (sold as Sea Bands), and extract of ginger taken by mouth. Anecdotal evidence suggests that they work, but scientific research has so far failed to prove it. However, they do no harm and might be worth a try.

As already mentioned, one of the best preventive measures is to avoid alcohol and in the case of people who have a tendency to suffer from motion sickness this avoidance should be for at least 24 hours prior to flying.

Chapter 5

Flying and Health

Every time you fly, your body has to re-adapt to the motions and conditions which are not normally experienced on the ground. To be a safe pilot you must be physically fit, psychologically sound and well trained. If you are unfamiliar with the medical factors which affect your performance in flight you are only partly trained to fly safely.

Regardless of how well you understand an aircraft and its systems and capabilities, and the vagaries of the weather, or how well you have mastered the skills and techniques of flight, if you suffer from slow responses, inattention, blunted judgement or are not capable of assessing your fitness to fly, you will be a hazard to yourself and others.

Although you may have achieved a first class pass in your last medical examination, that is now in the past; it is how fit you are today that matters, and you have to be able to determine your own physical and mental fitness before every flight if you are to meet your responsibilities as a safe pilot. This is one of the reasons why human performance and limitations have been introduced into the training syllabus for pilots. A good knowledge of physiological and psychological factors, and how they relate to your physical and mental performance, will help you to know when to fly and when not to.

Bear in mind that even a minor ailment such as a headache or cold can put you two or three degrees below your usual performance level, and while this might have little effect on your ability to conduct your day to day non-aviation tasks, it can seriously reduce your ability to handle safely the many piloting tasks vital to the well-being of yourself and your passengers. Ailments of any sort can produce distractions, and impair judgement, alertness and the ability to recall essential data and carry out calculations before and during flight.

Even when ailments are under control by medication, it may not only be the ailment that reduces your ability but also the actual medication.

Common ailments

Such ailments as the common cold, gastro-enteritis, diarrhoea, backache, and pains in the joints are usually temporary but can have a debilitating effect on your performance. Emotional upsets can have a powerful effect on your attitude of mind and you should avoid flying as a pilot while under emotional stress.

Legally, we all have a duty of care towards others and a pilot's primary responsibility is not just to fly an aircraft, but more importantly to ensure that every flight is made with maximum safety. Clearly to meet this requirement a pilot must be physically fit and mentally alert. Before you fly you should at least consider the following questions:

- Do I have a current medical certificate?
- Have I been taking medicine; if so, have there been any side effects?
- Am I worried or emotionally upset?
- When did I last have an alcoholic drink?
- Have I had a good night's sleep?
- Am I physically and mentally fit to operate an aircraft safely?

Depending on the circumstances there may be other points, but these would be a good start. Being fit helps to reduce tension and anxiety and increases self esteem. It has a favourable effect on emotions and should increase resistance to fatigue. Factors having a known influence on fitness include diet, exercise, stress levels and the use of tobacco, alcohol and drugs.

Head colds

Due to the risk of damage to the ear drums, aircrew should not fly in non-pressurised aircraft when they are suffering from head colds.

The way in which pressure in the middle ear is equalised with the outside atmosphere, via the Eustachian tube, was described in the previous chapter.

When a person suffers a head cold, the tissues of the mucous membrane inside the Eustachian tube (Fig. 5.1) swell, reducing the rate at which the air pressure equalises; this is particularly noticeable during descents. When the Eustachian tube is completely blocked by tissue swelling, and the rate of descent is sufficiently high, there maybe considerable pain and in certain cases the ear drum can be ruptured. This may be serious and can lead to a pilot losing his medical category.

Apart from the detrimental effects on the ear drum when flying with a head cold, there is also the effect on the sinus cavities. These are within the

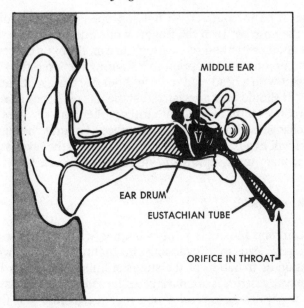

Fig. 5.1

bones of the face and skull and connected to the nose by narrow ducts lined with a mucous membrane. A head cold or hay fever can cause a partial or complete blockage of these ducts, which may result in considerable pain when descending to lower altitudes. Flying regularly with chronic catarrh can have serious consequences, often requiring an operation.

Sinus Cavities

Whenever someone is suffering from a head cold they should not fly in a non-pressurised aircraft. If a pilot or a passenger feels discomfort or pain during a descent, the rate of descent should be reduced or temporarily stopped to allow time for the air pressure outside and inside the ear drum to equalise.

Various methods can be used to help equalisation: chewing, yawning and swallowing will cause the small muscles around the nasal end of the

Eustachian tube to contract, so holding open the mouth of the tube. Pinching the nose between the fingers while building up pressure in the nostrils is another method of clearing the ears during a descent.

It is a common misconception that limiting the aircraft's altitude will enable a pilot with a head cold to fly without discomfort or damage to the ear drums. It should be appreciated that the rate of change in atmospheric pressure reduces with increase of altitude; therefore the greatest rate of pressure change will occur near the surface. To limit the flight to, say, 1000 ft agl will expose the pilot and passengers to the layer at which the pressure changes most rapidly during ascent or descent!

Stomach upsets

Another common ailment is a stomach upset, which can cause discomfort and pain and lead to distractions in flight. Gastritis, which is an inflammation or irritation of the stomach lining, can either be acute or chronic. Acute gastritis is often triggered by something you have drunk or eaten, so it pays to be careful about your diet before you fly. Chronic gastritis may persist for a long period, especially in older people, and may not be related to a particular diet. Gastro-enteritis may be a result of food poisoning and causes inflammation of the stomach lining and intestines. It is very disabling and can result in vomiting, diarrhoea, cramps and a raised temperature. Any of these should be a reason for you not to fly as a pilot. Gastric complaints are usually caused by bacterial or viral infections. Eating re-heated or partly cooked food is a very common cause.

Drugs, medicines and side effects

Alcohol

Aviation legislation is very strict in relation to alcohol before flying, and rightly so. In some countries the minimum period between drinking alcohol and flying is laid down very rigidly, whereas other countries tend to rely on basic statements, such as:

(1) A person shall not enter an aircraft when drunk, or be drunk in any aircraft.
(2) A person shall not, when acting as a member of the crew of any aircraft or being carried in any aircraft for the purpose of so acting, be under the influence of drink or a drug to such an extent as to impair his capacity so to act.

Even allowing for the legal wording, the message is quite clear. However, what is not quite so clear to an individual who has consumed alcohol, is whether it has impaired his performance as a member of flightcrew.

A review of accident reports over a long period has shown that alcohol was a primary or related factor in some aviation accidents. However, the number of accidents which had an alcohol connection represented a very small proportion of the total accidents each year. But it only needs one accident resulting in serious injury or loss of life, to make all pilots seriously consider the extent of the impairment to their performance which might result from drinking.

The relatively small number of alcohol related aviation accidents show that most pilots are only too well aware of the effects of alcohol on their personal performance in the cockpit. However, two basic problems will always exist for those pilots who are not total abstainers:

(1) Consumption of alcohol unfortunately means that the person concerned is unable to judge to what extent the alcohol has impaired judgement and ability. In other words, because of the nature of the effects of alcohol on the human brain, pilots may think they are not under the influence of alcohol when they are.

(2) It is difficult to know the length of time that should elapse before flight, in relation to the amount of alcohol consumed. To say 'Don't drink and fly' is to oversimplify. It is virtually impossible to lay down hard and fast rules without being unreasonable, because of the varying effects alcohol has on different people and on the same people at different times. It will be difficult for pilots to make correct decisions unless they understand the relationship between the consumption of alcohol and the effects on the brain and the body.

Effects of alcohol

Alcohol, whether in the form of beer or spirits, is a liquid known as ethyl alcohol, which acts as a depressant on the central nervous system. No one is immune from this effect. Alcohol for all practical purposes can be likened to an anaesthetic (Fig. 5.2).

When a person consumes alcohol it immediately begins to pass from the stomach into the bloodstream. The blood carries it to the brain where it initially affects the 'thinking cells', which control thinking, worrying and nervous reactions. In effect the process is similar to that caused by tranquillisers, and as a result a person becomes more relaxed and less prone to worry. Both these lead to a decrease in alertness.

The alcohol in the bloodstream then passes through the area of the brain that controls speech and muscle activity, with the result that speech and muscular co-ordination are adversely affected. If alcohol consump-

Fig. 5.2 Alcohol numbs the brain

tion is sufficiently high, the whole brain becomes affected and unconsciousness occurs (Fig. 5.3).

Alcohol is removed from the blood at a rate of approximately 15 milligrammes per 100 millilitres per hour. The consumption of 1½ pints of beer or three whiskies will result in a blood alcohol level of about 55–60 mgm/100 ml, and so it will take some four hours for the blood level to return to normal.

In most people alcohol initially causes euphoria and lessens inhibitions; even at low blood concentrations the risk of having an accident increases. Pilots' performance at tracking tasks requiring a moderate level of skill is affected at concentrations of 50 mgm/100 ml. For example, a group of pilots flying simulated instrument approaches were unable to meet the required performance levels after consuming the equivalent of 1½ pints of beer.

It is worth noting that some of the products of alcohol metabolism, by causing symptoms of a hangover, can also have a detrimental effect on performance. Regardless of popular belief, a person cannot speed up the rate at which alcohol leaves the body. The use of black coffee, steam baths or fresh air will not change the rate of oxidation, and sleeping off the effects of alcohol will actually cause the rate of oxidation to slow down because body functions are slowed during sleep. It should further be appreciated that although eating while drinking or drinking on a full stomach reduces the rate at which alcohol is absorbed into the bloodstream, it does not affect the rate at which oxidation occurs.

Another important point in relation to flying is that the effect of alcohol increases with altitude because alcohol interferes with the brain's ability to utilise oxygen. The effects are rapid because alcohol passes very quickly into the bloodstream, and the brain, being a highly vascular organ (a system of tiny channels), is immediately sensitive to changes in the

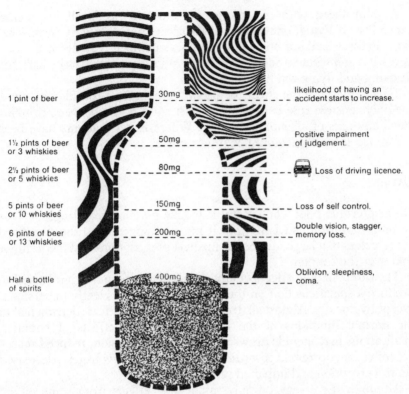

1 pint of beer	30mg	likelihood of having an accident starts to increase.
1½ pints of beer or 3 whiskies	50mg	Positive impairment of judgement.
2½ pints of beer or 5 whiskies	80mg	Loss of driving licence.
5 pints of beer or 10 whiskies	150mg	Loss of self control.
6 pints of beer or 13 whiskies	200mg	Double vision, stagger, memory loss.
Half a bottle of spirits	400mg	Oblivion, sleepiness, coma.

Fig. 5.3 Blood alcohol level

blood's composition. Therefore the oxygen concentration at altitude, coupled with the reduced capability of the brain to use the oxygen, all adds up to a serious impairment in the pilot's ability to think quickly and make correct decisions.

Because of all these factors and the varying effects that alcohol has on different people, it is not easy to give hard and fast rules on the quantity of drink consumed in relation to time allowed before flying. Recent in-flight research has confirmed that even in small uncomplicated aircraft, blood alcohol concentrations of 40 mgm/100 ml (half the legal driving limit) are associated with significant increases in errors committed by inexperienced and experienced pilots. From this it is clear that even a single alcoholic drink can produce a positive loss of performance, although the individual may not consider themselves to be affected.

It is also important to remember the after effects of alcohol on the semi-circular canals, with an increase in susceptibility to disorientation and motion sickness.

A pilot faced with an emergency situation needs all his mental capability. If flying, one should never accept any voluntary incapacitation. Before drinking any pilot should remember that drink is not a necessity, and whereas social drinking is in itself not necessarily harmful, drinking and flying can be lethal.

Finally, because the effects of alcohol remain for a considerable time, the only sensible rule is to allow at least eight hours between drinking small amounts of alcohol and flying. Where larger amounts have been consumed the period should be much longer.

Drugs

No responsible pilot would habitually take psychoactive drugs, such as heroin, marijuana and LSD, but it must be appreciated that the word 'drug' refers to a large number of medical prescriptions and medications sold over the counter.

The direct or side effects of any chemical compound administered to produce a specific action on the body are often not clearly understood, except by doctors. Almost all drugs have some side effects detrimental to the normal functions of the body. Major side effects of common medications may include drowsiness, mental depression, reduced sharpness of vision, decreased co-ordination, increased nervousness, decreased depth perception and impaired judgement.

Although there may be only minor side effects from some of the commonly used medications when a person is on the ground, these effects can be more subtle and unpredictable at altitude. Pilots must have a reasonable appreciation of this in order to judge when they are really fit to fly. However, any pilot who is undergoing treatment for an ailment is probably already unfit to fly, quite apart from the side effects of any medication.

Anti-histamines

Anti-histamine drugs are commonly used as cold cures and for the treatment of hay fever, asthma and allergic rashes. Many easily obtainable nose sprays and drops contain anti-histamines which can make a person drowsy and reduce the sense of balance and co-ordination. These side effects, together with the effects of the illness, will mean that a person is not fit to fly.

While very mild conditions of hay fever etc., may be adequately controlled by small doses of anti-allergic drugs before flying, a trial period on the ground is absolutely essential to establish whether there are any side effects. If in doubt, allow at least 24 hours after treatment involving anti-histamines before flying.

Pilots suffering from allergic conditions which require more than the absolute minimum treatment, and all who suffer from asthma, should not fly until they have consulted a doctor with experience in aviation medicine.

Sedatives and analgesics

Barbiturates, nerve tonics and pain killers are intended primarily to relieve anxiety or reduce pain. In doing so they normally suppress mental alertness. Fear and pain normally provide an essential alerting system; tranquillisers and sedatives suppress this and in the past have been a contributory cause to aircraft accidents. For this reason, pilots should not fly when taking this type of medication.

Amphetamines

Pep pills and weight reducing agents often contain amphetamines. Caffeine, dexedrine and benzedrine are used to keep people awake and can become habit forming. They act as a stimulant to the central nervous system, with the effect varying from one individual to another. In all cases they can cause dangerous overconfidence and can adversely affect a person's judgement, leading to reckless errors. Overdosage causes headaches, dizziness and mental disturbance. If coffee is not sufficient as a stimulant, you are not fit to fly – and remember that excessive coffee drinking itself may be harmful.

Antibiotics

Antibiotics such as penicillins and tetracyclines may have short term or delayed side effects which affect pilot performance. More importantly, their use usually indicates fairly severe infection and apart from any effect of the medication, the effects of the infection itself will almost always mean that the pilot is not fit to fly.

Anti-hypertensives

Drugs to relieve high blood pressure can cause a change in the mechanisms of blood circulation and an impairment of intellectual performance which could be disastrous when flying. If the blood pressure is such that drugs are needed the pilot must be temporarily grounded. Any treatment should be discussed with an expert in aviation medicine and clearance should be obtained from an authorised medical examiner before flying again.

Anaesthetics

Following local and general anaesthetics, including dental anaesthesia, at least 24 hours should elapse before returning to flying. This period will vary according to individual circumstances, and the dentist or anaesthetist should be asked for advice.

Analgesics

The more potent analgesics may have marked effects on performance. In any case, the pain for which they are being taken indicates that the person is not fit to fly.

Other medications

Many preparations now marketed contain a combination of medicines. It is essential therefore that if there is any change in medication or dosage, however slight, the pilot should wait and see if there are any effects while on the ground before attempting to fly. Although the above are the common medicines that produce adverse effects on pilot performance, many other forms of medication may do so in individuals who are 'oversensitive' to that particular preparation. If you are in any doubt ask a doctor experienced in aviation medicine.

If you are ill and need treatment, do make sure the doctor knows you are a pilot or flightcrew member and whether you have recently been abroad.

Drugs of addiction

Drugs of addiction cover a wide field, including morphine, hypnotics, tranquillisers, heroin and marijuana. All have a basic effect of 'detaching' the person from the realities of their environment. This is not compatible with control of an aircraft and a person using them is not fit to be a member of a flightcrew.

Precautions

A pilot should be cautious of taking 'over the counter' remedies. If uncertain about taking a particular medicine before or during flight, consult an authorised aviation medical examiner.

Although the most common drugs which adversely affect pilot performance have been mentioned in this chapter, remember that there are many other forms of medication which can affect individuals who are sensitive to them. Pilots must therefore avoid taking any drugs or medicines before or during flight unless completely familiar with the side effects and certain that their flying ability will not be impaired.

Remember, too, that the need for medication implies the presence of an illness, and if a pilot is ill he has no more business in the air than a rough running engine or other malfunctioning piece of equipment. The safest rule is to take no medication before or during flight unless one has obtained the go-ahead from an authorised aviation medical examiner. Not only might the medication dull a pilot's alertness but it might suppress the symptoms of the illness, making a pilot feel better than he or she really is and so leading to situations where lack of sound judgement causes an accident.

It should also be borne in mind that the combination of two drugs taken at the same time may render both more potent, or cause side effects not experienced with each individual medicine.

Donation of blood

Donating blood is incompatible with flying. The circulation takes several weeks to return completely to normal and although effects are slight at ground level, there are risks when flying. Pilots are recommended not to volunteer as blood donors; if blood has been given an appropriate doctor should be consulted before returning to flying.

Fatigue and tiredness

It is convenient to differentiate between fatigue, which is objective, and tiredness, which is mainly subjective. With fatigue, performance is usually affected due to physiological changes involving nervous and muscular activities. Tiredness or sleepiness, on the other hand, may be due to boredom or other psychological factors and can therefore occur without true fatigue. When tired, it is possible to respond adequately to increased flight demands, for example a difficult instrument approach, by increasing one's state of alertness. This may not be possible with true fatigue.

Performance will depend on the degree of fatigue but clearly a fatigued pilot should not be in command of an aircraft as his or her reactions will be slow and this reduced mental altertness can lead to dangerous situations both in the planning stage or during the flight. Some degree of fatigue will, however, always be present during physical or mental effort such as when flying an aircraft. However, the effects can be kept within reasonable bounds by maintaining a good state of physical fitness and by proper planning to reduce cockpit workloads to a reasonable level during flight.

Because of the importance of remaining alert and reacting quickly and correctly when airborne, a pilot should understand the causes of fatigue and take precautions to reduce its effect on his or her performance in the cockpit. Fatigue falls into two broad categories:

(1) chronic fatigue;
(2) acute fatigue.

Chronic fatigue extends over a long period and often has a psychological cause. It can be brought on by continuous strain due to domestic or work pressures, or an underlying disease. Fatigue of this type can also be responsible for physical discomfort such as stomach disorders, intestinal problems and general aches and pains throughout the body. It can also lead to emotional illness. Any pilot suffering from this type of fatigue should consult a doctor and should at all costs avoid flying as a pilot until the condition is cured.

Acute fatigue is usually short-lived and is accepted as a normal part of everyday life. It is a weariness felt after excitement, lack of sleep, the effects of unusually loud noise or after a period of strenuous activity. Relaxing or sleeping are the normal cures for this condition. Causes most commonly associated with flying are:

- The physical stresses imposed by flying an aircraft in turbulent air, concentration on instrument flying and the handling problems which arise when aircraft equipment malfunctions etc.
- A deficiency of oxygen.
- Psychological stress, either from emotional causes or resulting from periods of demanding intellectual activity. Sustained psychological stress will normally result in the production of the hormones which prepare the body for quick reactions. These substances cause the respiratory and circulatory systems of the body to work at a faster rate than normal, thus making the liver release energy to provide the additional fuel needed for extra brain and muscle activity. Their energy is limited and once the supply is depleted the body lapses into a state of significant fatigue.

Fatigue may be compounded by what is called the 'arousal state'. A person's performance is directly related to this state, an aspect which is covered later in Chapter 10.

Sleep and fatigue

A pilot cannot operate efficiently if suffering from fatigue, because of the reduced alertness. Conditions relating to fatigue are also brought about by daily cyclical changes in the body, such as temperature and wakefulness. Changes of this type are called circadian rhythms (circa, around; dia, day).

Body functions are thought to be controlled by internal, 'biological' clocks. While the mechanisms of these clocks are largely unknown, their effects are familiar to everyone. Waking, sleeping, eating and elimination of wastes are regular everyday human experiences. Most people also note daily periods of alertness and periods of dullness. These are normal and are related to swings of 1° to 2° in body temperature. People are most alert when the body temperature is highest and least alert when it is lowest.

For people who sleep at night and work in the daytime, the body's low temperature point occurs around 3 am to 5 am. It is at this time that they are most prone to errors. Studies of pilots confirm that performance failures and human error accidents are most likely to occur early in the morning.

High speed long-range aircraft are now commonplace, both in the commercial transport sector and in general aviation. Crews on such aircraft can be subjected to rapid time zone displacement when travelling east or west. Jet lag, or desynchronosis, means that travellers' body functions remain on home time and do not occur at the same times as those of residents at the destination; for example, the traveller gets sleepy or hungry at inappropriate times.

If the traveller stays at the destination long enough, the biological clock will gradually become reset to the new time. This re-setting, or entrainment, takes place on average at the rate of approximately one hour per day for each time zone crossed, but this will vary from person to person.

This means that if a pilot flies from New York to London (six time zones), about six days will be required for the body functions to adjust to the local time in London. The same re-adjustment will be needed by a pilot flying from London to New York, though it will be less difficult because it is easier to stretch the day (east to west flight) than it is to compress the day (west to east flight).

However, in either case a pilot may be flying at a time of 'circadian low' and should be aware that he or she is more prone to errors at that time. Sticking strictly to printed checklists is the main insurance against error. Two heads are better than one: one pilot should read out the items and the other should check them, with only clearly spoken responses accepted. Pilots flying alone should read and respond aloud to all checklist items.

Precautions against fatigue

- Obtain adequate sleep before any flight. When a body is resting, its store of energy is being replenished.
- Stick to a reasonably balanced diet and have regular meals. This prevents the body from consuming its stores to supply energy.

- Maintain good physical condition. The right amount of exercise helps to keep the body fit and healthy, and a fit body is less susceptible to fatigue.
- When single pilot operations are conducted, keep the stage lengths of any flight to no more than 3 or 4 hours.
- One contribution to fatigue is posture, particularly during longish flights. Pilots should always take reasonable care that their seats are adjusted correctly to give maximum comfort.

- Pilots who will not be at their destination long enough to adapt to local time, should remain on home time in their activities. In extreme cases this can mean daytime sleep and breakfast at night, but it will to some extent prevent fatigue resulting from insomnia. People experiencing jet lag can force themselves to carry out activities such as going to meetings, shopping, etc., but they cannot force themselves to sleep when they are not sleepy. Tourists lying awake all night and then dragging themselves about sightseeing the next day are a fairly trivial example; however, such a situation could be a significant problem for a pilot, who must be in top form for a flight.

  Pilots should never take sedative drugs, including alcohol, in an attempt to cope with jet lag or insomnia. Equally, the use of stimulants such as amphetamines in an attempt to be 'up' at the time of a circadian low period should be strictly avoided. The adverse effects far outweigh any alleged benefits. Pilots should also remember that the effects of drugs can wear off during flight, leaving the pilot in a worse condition than he or she might have been in otherwise.
- Passengers on scheduled medication who are experiencing jet lag should continue to take their medicine on home time, otherwise doses may be either too close together or too far apart.
- Departure times are usually selected to fit in with desired arrival times, such as for scheduled meetings, hotel reservations, etc. Weather forecasts may also have powerful influences. The result may be a departure or arrival scheduled at a time of circadian low, when the likelihood of human error is greatest. At such time errors of confusion and forgetfulness are most common. 'Forcing functions' such as checklists, warning horns, stick shakers, flags and lights are most important in combating reduced alertness. Pre-flight procedures

should always include checks to see that these safety features are operating according to specifications.

The flightcrew medical examination

Standards

The standards for physical fitness of aircrew are laid down by the International Civil Aviation Organisation, but slight variations are made by different licensing authorities. The standards are not prohibitively exacting and do not refer to fitness as much as lack of illness. It might be helpful, therefore, to look at the aircrew medical examination to give some idea of what the authorised medical examiner is looking for.

(1) *Height and weight* These measurements are taken so that any obesity may be assessed. Although obesity is a known risk factor in the development of heart disease, it is very rare for anyone to lose their medical certificate up to 50% above ideal body weight.

(2) *Vision* This is assessed to ensure that the individual has safe sight with each eye, both for distant and close work. As described in Chapter 3, almost all the normal visual difficulties which occur with ageing can be corrected with lenses and cause no licensing problems. Individuals who develop cataracts are now allowed to hold a licence after surgery and the installation of plastic lens implants.

Circulation occurs in and out of the eye structure. Glaucoma is a condition in which the normal outflow of fluid is restricted, leading to a build-up of intraocular pressure within the eyeball. This may lead to visual impairment if not treated, and this can be disqualifying.

(3) *Hearing* The hearing loss which is allowed for even a professional licence medical certificate is very generous. Few pilots will approach critical levels of deafness, particularly in both ears, and pilots who do fail to meet the standards may still be assessed as fit if they pass a practical hearing test.

(4) *Urine analysis* The urine is examined primarily to detect protein, which may indicate some form of kidney disease, and sugar, which may be an indication of diabetes. It should be stressed that the test done in the surgery is only a screen, and if any abnormality is indicated further tests are necessary.

Kidney disease is rarely a problem and can usually be treated without any restriction on the licence.

Diabetes is relatively common and is a condition in which sugars and starch are not properly utilised due to a deficiency in the hormones produced by the pancreas. It may be in one of two basic forms: one requires insulin injections for the control of blood sugar, and the other can be managed by diet or diet plus tablets.

Many individuals who show a diabetic tendency with sugar in the urine can control the situation by maintaining ideal body weight and eating an appropriate diet. They can hold a flying licence. However, if tablets or injections are required to control the blood sugar, this is disqualifying.

(5) *Blood pressure measurement*   High blood pressure, or hypertension, rarely causes symptoms of which the individual is aware and is usually only discovered during a medical examination. It is of concern because of its close association with heart disease and strokes. Consequently, upper limits have been laid down which are of the order of 160 mmHg systolic and 100 mmHg diastolic. The systolic pressure is that necessary for the cuff to completely stop the blood flow in the artery in the upper limb, and equates to the pressure in the arteries as the heart contracts. The diastolic pressure is that in the cuff which allows the blood to flow in the artery when the heart is relaxing between beats.

Blood pressure varies throughout the day and is affected by physical and emotional states. Thus a single high reading is not usually considered significant, but repeated high readings will indicate that some action is necessary.

The usual first steps are reduction to ideal weight, possibly salt restriction, a gentle exercise programme, and no alcohol. The individual will also be strongly advised to give up smoking, as it gives an added risk of heart disease.

The next step is control by drugs. Although many of these in use have significant side effects, there are some which will allow the individual to hold an aircrew licence.

(6) *The electrocardiogram (ECG)*   This records the electrical activity of the heart muscle. It shows the heart rhythm and the order in which different parts of the heart are contracting. It also gives some indication of the condition of the heart muscle and can sometimes show evidence of damage due to poor blood supply.

Maintenance of personal fitness

The commonest cause of licence loss is related to the cardiovascular system, often resulting from the formation of fatty deposits on the inside of the blood vessels (atheroma), leading to a poor oxygen supply to the tissues. If the affected tissue is the heart, this leads to angina or to a heart attack. If the affected tissue is the brain, the result is a transient ischaemic attack (TIA) or, more seriously, a stroke. These conditions can cause personality change, a decrease in intellectual capacity or fits, as well as the better known symptoms and signs of a stroke.

Risk factors associated with blood vessel disease are listed below, but they are only a general guide. There is always an exception to any rule or advice and we can only work with probabilities and averages. You will improve your chances of continuing good health however, if you take into account that the following risk factors are known to be important in the incidence of blood vessel disease:

(1) *Age and family history.* Nothing can be done about these!

(2) *High blood pressure.* Persistent hypertension is associated with increased disease, which is why such importance is placed on regular monitoring.

(3) *Diabetes.* Individuals with a diabetic tendency have an increased risk of cardiovascular disease.

(4) *Obesity.* This is a risk in its own right as well as pre-disposing to high blood pressure.

(5) *Blood fats.* Cholesterol level appears to be related to cardiovascular disease. It can often be brought down dramatically by altering the diet. Other blood fats are also thought to be important.

(6) *Inactivity.* Lack of physical exercise contributes to atheroma. Everybody should put their heart rate into the 'training range' for 20 minutes two or three times per week. To find your training pulse rate, subtract your age from 220. This gives your maximum heart rate, and your training range is 60% to 80% of this.

However, beware. If you do not normally take exercise, work up to regular exercise gradually and under supervision.

(7) *Tobacco.* Use of this drug is heavily implicated in the formation of atheroma. It also causes constriction of the small blood vessels, compounding the problems of inadequate blood flow. This is thought to be one of the most important factors in the development of coronary artery disease.

(8) *Caffeine.* Excessive caffeine intake can be a factor in developing cardiovascular disease. It has been suggested that caffeine beverages should be limited to a maximum of four cups per day.

As with all things in life, the answer is moderation coupled with awareness of the risks.

Chapter 6

Passenger Care

Passengers come in all shapes, sizes and temperaments. It is not unknown for a pilot to take up a friend who is normally a calm, relaxed individual, only to find that he or she becomes completely unnerved and panicky during some flight mishap or even in uneventful flight.

Everyone operates at two psychological levels – the rational and the emotional. A person's daily activities are regulated by rational forces: logic, knowledge, experience and motivation. However, underlying these elements certain emotions lie dormant, such as fear, anger or frustration.

Anxiety

Fear, or more accurately anxiety, is the emotion most often felt by passengers during flight. Many have some vague anxiety about what might happen if things go wrong, and in a minor incident they react like any human being in danger. Most try to remain calm while enduring an inner torment and tension. This may be apparent from heavy perspiring, stony silence, chain smoking, rambling conversation or other odd behaviour, all of which often leads to greater anxiety.

Another consideration is that if you are carrying several passengers and one displays anxiety, it can quickly spread to others. Any group of panicky passengers could well be a threat to the safety of the flight and at best will become a distracting influence to the pilot, particularly in the close confines of a small aircraft cabin.

Passenger care should start on the ground before the flight. When the flight is purely for pleasure in the local area, you should first consider the suitability of the weather. Strong gusty winds or marked turbulence are definitely not suitable conditions for local pleasure flights, as apart from the increased risk of motion sickness, passengers are more likely to become anxious.

Safety briefing

The next step is to ensure that your passengers are briefed properly on matters affecting their personal safety and that of the aircraft. This briefing should include:

Smoking
Whether or not you allow smoking during flight will depend on your personal wishes and whether it is legally permitted in the particular aircraft. If smoking is permitted ensure passengers know where the ashtrays are. Bear in mind that a dropped cigarette will often roll to an inaccessible and flammable spot, creating an anxious situation for both yourself and your passengers. In any event, smoking should at least be prohibited during take-off and landing, during fuelling operations and at all times in the vicinity of the aircraft on the ground.

Adjustment of seats
Explain to passengers how to adjust their seats and ensure they are securely locked in position. If this is not done, in the event of an emergency valuable time could be wasted by passengers who do not know how to slide their seats rearwards, to enable quicker evacuation from the aircraft.

If the aircraft seats have adjustable backs this too should be explained and the passengers briefed that the fully upright position must be used when taking-off or landing.

Safety harness or belts
The pilot should ensure that these are correctly fastened before each flight, and that the passengers know how to fit them properly. Harnesses

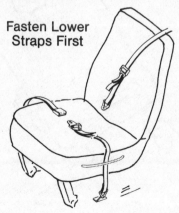

Fasten Lower
Straps First

made up of a non-inertial and upper torso restraining straps should be adjusted by first tightening the lap straps and only then pulling the upper strap(s) tight. If the upper strap(s) are pulled tight first, the lap straps will be lifted up across the body and in a heavy impact there would be a danger of the wearer slipping down and forward through the harness.

It would also be advisable to suggest that passengers keep their safety harnesses or belts fastened at all times during the flight.

Location and operation of doors and emergency exits
In certain emergencies it will be vital for the passengers to exit quickly. Therefore it is imperative, on safety grounds, for them to know how to operate doors, canopies and emergency exits. The operation of all these varies from aircraft to aircraft; one has only to consider the flush mounted tab and separate lock of a Cessna 150, the swinging arm rest lever of the Cessna 172, the various button and handle combinations of other aircraft and the latching systems of the different canopies, to appreciate the variety of mechanisms used. A similar variety of emergency exits exists, so it is essential that passengers are adequately briefed on how to operate doors, canopies and all emergency exits.

Use of flotation devices
When flying over water, responsible pilots will ensure that flotation equipment is carried. However, this will be no use if a few minutes before

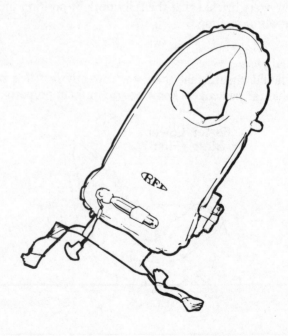

a ditching the passengers have to start reading instructions on how to use it.

When planning a flight over water review ditching procedures with your passengers and when practical demonstrate their use, paying specific attention to how and when items such as lifejackets should be inflated.

The use of oxygen equipment

When the intention is to fly at altitudes which may require the use of oxygen, passengers must be briefed before flight on the correct procedures. This applies to both pressurised and non-pressurised aircraft.

Passengers will need to know about such standard precautions as removing lipstick and not smoking when oxygen is in use, and they must be instructed on how to plug in and adjust their masks. Bear in mind that at altitudes of 20,000 feet or more the time of useful consciousness is very short; for example at 24,000 feet it is about three minutes. The onset of hypoxia is insidious and passengers should be made aware of the warning symptoms of lack of oxygen.

A pilot who has to cope with loss of pressurisation or the failure of oxygen equipment will be well occupied handling the emergency and getting the aircraft down to a lower altitude; there will be little time to sort out oxygen problems among passengers.

Approach to briefing

When carrying out your passenger briefing display a relaxed attitude and avoid giving the impression that accidents and emergencies are commonplace. Stress that the briefing is a precaution, designed to make passengers more aware of their surroundings so they are comfortable and can relax in confidence without the fear of the unknown troubling them during flight.

In flight

During the flight itself keep manoeuvres smooth, avoiding sudden and abrupt aircraft movements. You will need to keep a watchful eye on your passengers' activities in the aircraft, as well as maintaining a good supply of fresh air in the cabin and paying particular attention to any early signs of discomfort or nausea. If you are carrying first time fliers, whenever practical stay reasonably close to your aerodrome of departure so that you can make a fairly rapid return should they begin to show signs of becoming unwell or unduly anxious.

Finally, keep in mind that the various medical aspects previously discussed in this manual also apply to your passengers. With this knowledge and your own confidence and control over the flight, along with awareness of your passengers' needs and possible reactions to flying, a relaxed and safe flight should result.

Personal hygiene

Personal hygiene can be a delicate subject. Nevertheless this section of the manual would not be complete without a brief mention, particularly to point out that, in the close confinement of a cockpit, body and breath odours can be very unpleasant for other occupants.

Personal cleanliness is essential if you want to share your flying with others. It is clearly very frustrating to have spent much effort and money learning to be a good pilot, if no one wants to fly with you because of personal hygiene problems.

If you normally smoke during flight, it would be advisable not to do so when you have passengers on board. Aircraft cockpits and small cabin aircraft are fairly confined and non-smokers are often upset by tobacco fumes. If you must have an occasional smoke during a long flight, it would at least show courtesy to your passengers if you first asked whether they object.

Appearance and habits

While on the subject of hygiene, there is the closely related consideration of personal appearance and habits. The respect and confidence of others has to be earned and it is advisable to start with a professional appearance. Appearing neat, clean and appropriately dressed is important, as are personal habits and mannerisms, when seeking the respect that should be given to a pilot in command.

Other people's respect for you and trust in you will be undermined if you show tenseness, thoughtlessness, inattentiveness, erratic movements, distracting speech habits or capricious changes of mood. You should develop and maintain a calm, thoughtful, attentive and disciplined image. Keep in mind that when emergencies occur in flight, it is the pilot in command who shoulders the responsibility for the safety of the aircraft's occupants. Without their full co-operation in following the pilot's instructions, chaos leading to an even greater emergency can result.

Chapter 7

Toxic Hazards

Articles or substances capable of posing significant risks to health, safety or property, when carried in an aircraft, are classified as dangerous goods. They can threaten safety, particularly when carried in aircraft with small cabins.

Today, numerous potentially dangerous materials are produced by industry and used by the general public. For example, hydrocyanic acid – an extremely toxic agent – is commonly used in dyes, fumigants and plastics and can be found in plastic furnishings. In a fire it could produce a lethal gas. Clearly, pilots cannot be expected to have a degree in chemistry, but awareness and common sense will normally enable them to recognise the potential dangers of many items which could be loaded or carried on to an aircraft.

Substances which are corrosive or flammable should be avoided, particularly in liquid form. It is also important to remember that certain fire extinguishers can produce toxic fumes. Many older types of aircraft were originally equipped with carbon tetrachloride extinguishers. These are no longer permitted because they produce phosgene gas and other highly toxic vapours, although some can still be found. Pilots should avoid using them and have them replaced with BCF or CO_2 extinguishers.

Flammable goods which may be carried in reasonable safety by other forms of transport can present extreme hazards in an aircraft hold or cabin as the aircraft occupants will be unable to leave the confined space of the aircraft until it has landed.

Dangerous goods

Pilots must therefore appreciate the potential hazard of certain articles, including:

- explosives of any nature;
- flammable liquids and solids including such items as paint removers,

liquid flavouring extracts, paints and varnishes, petrol, thinners, alcohol, matches and firelighters;

- oxidising materials, e.g. nitrates that yield oxygen readily, which may in turn stimulate combustion;
- corrosive liquids, such as battery acids, mercury, certain cleaning compounds and similar agents;
- compressed gases including most household sprays.

To appreciate the care necessary, one has only to consider the potential effects of one commonly used household item, an aerosol can. This, or any other item packaged under pressure, represents a hazard when carried in an aircraft because the outside air pressure lowers substantially with increasing altitude. This could result in the aerosol cannister exploding and the contents catching fire.

With this in mind, remember that it is the pilot in command of an aircraft who is ultimately responsible for compliance with the regulations and the safety of any flight.

Carbon monoxide

Apart from articles carried on board, there is the possible hazard of carbon monoxide. This is produced by incomplete combustion of any carbonaceous substance. It is always present in the exhaust fumes of aero piston engines and also in tobacco smoke. Although carbon monoxide is colourless, odourless, and tasteless, it is often associated with gases and fumes which can be detected by smell and sight.

Effects

The effect of inhaling this poisonous gas can be extremely serious, starting with headache, nausea, dizziness and reduction in vision, and leading to vomiting, loss of muscular power, unconsciousness and death.

When carbon monoxide is taken into the lungs it combines with the oxygen carrying pigment (haemoglobin) of the blood cells. Haemoglobin has an affinity for carbon monoxide two hundred times greater than its affinity for oxygen (Fig. 7.1). Therefore if there were one part of carbon monoxide to two hundred parts of oxygen in an aircraft cabin, the haemoglobin of the pilot's and passengers' blood would attract the same amount of each.

If a larger proportion of carbon monoxide were present in the air being breathed, it would virtually prevent any oxygen being attracted to the blood cells, and the human body would suffer oxygen starvation. This would result in the brain becoming deprived of its essential supply of oxygen, and a person's ability to think and reason would diminish rapidly.

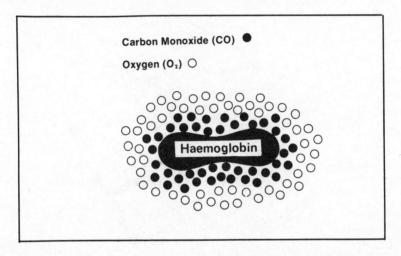

Fig. 7.1 Carbon monoxide (CO) affinity is much stronger than oxygen (O_2)

Short exposure to relatively high concentrations of carbon monoxide will seriously affect a pilot's ability to operate an aircraft. The same effects will result if the pilot is exposed to lower concentrations for longer periods. A practical and very important fact is that because carbon monoxide effects are cumulative, a pilot who flies several times in the same day or on successive days in an aircraft with carbon monoxide concentrations, can eventually suffer serious effects.

Unlike hypoxia which can be rapidly remedied by a few deep breaths of oxygen, carbon monoxide poisoning may take days or weeks to recover from because the carbon monoxide attaches itself tenaciously to the haemoglobin. Susceptibility to carbon monoxide also increases with altitude because as air pressure decreases so too does the amount of oxygen being passed into the blood cells through the lungs. Tobacco smoke also produces carbon monoxide so smoking will introduce more carbon monoxide into the body.

Cabin heating systems

The most common cause of carbon monoxide in an aircraft is a defective
cabin heating system. Most light aircraft have heating systems which
produce air from heat exchangers that use heat from exhaust gases (Fig.
7.2). Any cracks or defects in the heat exchanger system permit
concentrations of carbon monoxide to enter the cabin and be breathed by
the occupants. Carbon monoxide can also enter a cabin through openings
in the engine compartment firewall and other access points, e.g. windows.

Fig. 7.2

Detection methods

Adequate aircraft inspection and maintenance are the primary precautions. Concentrations of carbon monoxide exceeding one part in 20,000
parts of air can become hazardous in the aircraft cabin. To prevent this a
thorough examination of the exhaust manifold and cabin heating system
should be conducted at regular intervals. Carbon monoxide in the cabin
or the cockpit has been traced to worn or defective exhaust stack slip
joints, exhaust system cracks or holes, openings in the engine firewall,
'blowby' at the engine breather, defective gaskets in the exhaust manifold,
defective mufflers, and inadequate sealing of fairings around strut fittings
on the fuselage.

When an aircraft is being operated on a Public Transport Certificate of
Airworthiness, the inspections required under the maintenance schedule
will normally be sufficient to reveal any of the above defects. However in
the case of aircraft operated on a Private Category Certificate of

Airworthiness or on a Special Category, there are no statutory inspection periods with the exception of the annual checks, and the pilot may be allowed to carry out certain periodic inspections himself. In this situation the pilot needs to be particularly alert to the condition of the cabin heating system.

Regular inspections of cabin heating systems can be supplemented with carbon monoxide detectors. There are two types available. One determines the carbon monoxide content of the air by drawing a small sample of air into a transparent tube containing material which changes colour according to the amount of carbon monoxide present. A colour chart showing the different levels is supplied with the equipment. The other, more simple type of detector consists of a small porous disc mounted on a plastic plate. This disc contains a chemical which changes colour on contact with carbon monoxide. The porous disc is exposed to the cabin air for a specific time, then compared with the colour reading on the instruction card. Although this type of detector is not as accurate as the air sampler system, it has the advantage of being simple and inexpensive yet reasonably efficient.

Symptoms of carbon monoxide poisoning

All pilots must be aware of the symptoms of carbon monoxide poisoning:

(1) a feeling of sluggishness, of being too warm, and a tightness across the forehead;
(2) throbbing pressure in the temples and ringing in the ears;
(3) severe headache, general weakness, dizziness and dimming of vision;
(4) larger amounts of carbon monoxide in the body will result in a loss of muscular power, vomiting, weakening of the pulse rate and a slowing down of the respiratory rate.

Precautions
If a pilot smells exhaust fumes or begins to feel any of the above symptoms he should assume that carbon monoxide is present in the cabin air and take the following steps:

(1) immediately shut off the cabin air heater and close any other opening which might be conveying air from the engine into the cabin;
(2) open all normal sources of 'fresh air' to the cabin (including windows if permissible);
(3) avoid smoking;
(4) if oxygen is available it should be inhaled by the occupants of the cabin;
(5) if the symptoms of carbon monoxide poisoning occur during flight

the pilot should land at the first reasonable opportunity and carry out carbon monoxide checks on the aircraft before resuming the flight.

The winter months, when cabin heating systems are most commonly used, will normally be the time of greatest risk from carbon monoxide. It is always advisable to have fresh air vents open whenever the cabin heating system is being used. Although this will not prevent carbon monoxide entering the cabin, it will dilute the quantity if it is present.

Chapter 8

Incapacitation During Flight

Certain pathological conditions have, to a varying degree, been a factor in some aviation accidents or incidents. While incapacitation of one flightcrew member can normally be handled during multicrew operations, greater difficulties obviously arise when the flight crew comprises only one pilot, as is the case in most general aviation flights.

In-flight incapacitation may be partial or total. Partial incapacitation may not be detected easily, even by the person affected. Any form of physical pain or discomfort can lead to a deterioration in mental performance with a subsequent detrimental effect on a pilot's ability to make good judgements and sensible decisions. There are numerous causes of some degree of incapacitation during flight:

- gastro-intestinal disorders;
- stress, fatigue, lack of sleep, disruption of circadian rhythm, dieting, etc.;
- blocked sinuses causing pain, particularly during rapid descents;
- congestion in the Eustachian tubes, causing pain during descents;
- carbon monoxide in the cabin;
- lack of oxygen;
- bladder problems, urinary infection, kidney stone attack;
- cardiovascular problems, heart disease or attacks;
- the side effects of medication.

Precautions against many of these have already been covered in this manual. Nevertheless there still remains the question of how to manage the situation should in-flight incapacitation occur.

Any advice can only be in the broadest terms because of the varying circumstances which could apply. Apart from the common sense actions of conducting 'stair-step' descents in the case of sinus or ear pain, and the use of oxygen (if available) to assist any form of breathing problem, dizziness or nausea, the two most sensible actions are to discontinue the flight as soon as safely possible by proceeding to the nearest aerodrome, and at the same time to communicate with ATC giving details of the situation. This advice would also apply in the event of passenger incapacitation. If the passenger or second crew member concerned is seated in the front of the aircraft, it is important to ensure that his or her upper torso restraint is tightened sufficiently to prevent any bodily collapse on to the flying controls.

Scuba diving and flying

Any pilot or passenger who intends to fly after scuba diving should allow their body sufficient time to get rid of excess nitrogen absorbed during diving. If they do not, decompression sickness from dissolved gas coming out of solution can occur at even low altitudes and can create a serious in-flight problem. This is true whether flying in a non-pressurised or pressurised aircraft. Bear in mind that in the case of the latter the cabin pressure is maintained at a pressure altitude of approximately 8000 feet above sea level.

The recommended waiting time before flight to a cabin pressure altitude of up to 8000 feet is at least 12 hours after diving which has not required controlled ascent (non-decompression diving), and at least 24 hours after diving which has required controlled descent (de-compression diving). The waiting time before flight to cabin pressure altitudes above 8000 feet should be at least 24 hours following any scuba diving.

To sum up

In exercising your responsibilities as a pilot you should comply with your duty of care to your passengers, yourself and other people in the air and on the ground. Before attempting any flight ask yourself: 'Am I physically and mentally fit to fly?' You can only answer Yes, I'M SAFE, if you are not impaired by:

> **I**llness
> **M**edication
> **S**tress
> **A**lcohol
> **F**atigue
> **E**motion

Chapter 9

First Aid

Although this first part of the manual deals mainly with physiological aspects, it would not really be complete without some information on first aid. Private pilots are not expected to be skilled first aiders, but they should have a rudimentary knowledge of how to handle injured persons following an accident to their aircraft.

This section deals with basic matters which may arise in the event of injury to passengers following an incident such as a forced landing, when medical assistance or a qualified first aider are not immediately available. More detailed and practical knowledge of first aid can be obtained by studying the Red Cross or St. John Ambulance Association's manuals, or preferably by taking one of the short courses run by these and similar organisations.

Procedures following an accident

The basic check list for all first aid is A, B, C.

A – check that the Airway is clear;
B – stop the Bleeding by direct pressure;
C – check the blood Circulation and begin artificial respiration if necessary.

If a passenger has been injured, the first point is to ensure as far as possible that there is no further potential danger, e.g. fire. The injuries suffered by an aircraft occupant can be broadly divided as follows:

- fractured or broken limbs;
- severe bleeding;
- head injuries;
- severe shock;
- burns.

The passenger may have suffered more than one of these and may be conscious and capable of moving, or unconscious and immobile.

Immediate actions

An instinctive reaction is to start pulling injured people out of the aircraft. However, this may increase injuries or worse, so the first action (unless there is a threat of fire or similar danger) is to determine the extent of the person's injuries. This will naturally be more difficult in the case of an unconscious person, when it is better, if possible, to leave them where they are until medical assistance arrives. However, if the casualty is severely shocked (see later in this chapter) it may be necessary to lie them down to improve the blood supply to the brain, in which case they may have to be removed from the aircraft.

If it is necessary to move an unconscious person, try to give adequate support to all parts of the body, particularly the neck and spine, and avoid jerky movements when easing them out of the aircraft cabin. The casualty should be carried to the nearest safe area, still supporting the neck and back, and laid down in the 'recovery position', shown in Fig. 9.1. This position provides the necessary stability to keep the casualty as comfortable as possible, and with the head turned to one side it reduces the possibility of asphyxia if vomiting occurs.

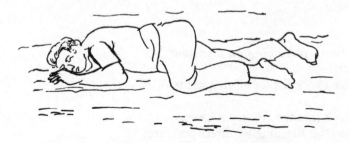

Fig. 9.1

When moving a conscious injured person bear in mind that if they are severely injured or shocked they may not feel pain. You should ascertain whether they are suffering from a numbing or tingling sensation in the arms and legs, to determine whether they are injured and where. Remember that the casualty may not be capable of giving very accurate answers so care must be taken when assisting them out of the aircraft cabin.

When moving an injured passenger, whether conscious or unconscious, remember to ensure first the clearest access possible and then handle the casualty very gently, with minimum movement of the neck and spine.

Fractured or broken limbs

These should, where possible, be immobilised before the casualty is moved. Splints may be improvised from items avilable such as walking sticks, pieces of wood, cardboard or a firmly folded magazine. Use bandages, handkerchiefs or similar to strap the splint into position along

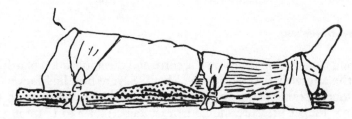

Fig. 9.2

the limb. The splint should immobilise the joint either side of the fracture, and where possible some padding should be placed between the limb and the splint (Fig. 9.2). Always tie the knots on the outside of the splint, to prevent further damage to the limb or discomfort to the casualty. Check at intervals of approximately 15 minutes to ensure that the bandages are not becoming too tight as a result of swelling of the injured tissues.

Fig. 9.3

If no material for a splint is available and the injury is to a lower limb, the undamaged leg can be bound to the injured one using three broad bandages or strips of material as shown in Fig. 9.3.

When a thigh has been fractured apply a well padded splint between the limbs and an extra long padded splint to the side of the injured limb.

This splint should extend from the armpit to the foot, as shown in Figure 9.4. Immobilise the limbs with two extra bandages, one against the pelvis in line with the hip joints and the other around the chest just below the armpits.

Fig. 9.4

Severe bleeding

Bleeding usually stops of its own accord, and the application of a dressing from the aircraft's first aid box will help. Severe bleeding however will need more action such as pressure to the bleeding point on top of the dressing. Finger pressure should be maintained for 5 to 15 minutes, and when the wound is relatively large the pressure should close the sides of the wound firmly together.

Keep the casualty still and apply fresh dressings as required. Where possible the injured part should be raised and immobilised, either with a sling if it is an upper limb or by tying the legs together if it is a lower limb.

If bleeding cannot be controlled by pressure to the wound, or if it is impossible to apply direct pressure successfully, a 'pressure point' between the wound and the heart will have to be used. A pressure point is a position where an artery can be compressed against the underlying bone to stem the flow of blood (Fig. 9.5). This pressure should not normally be maintained for more than 15 minutes.

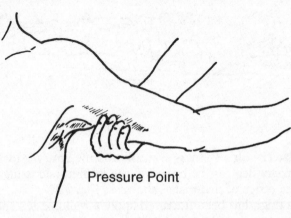

Pressure Point

Fig. 9.5

Head injuries

Apart from surface damage and bleeding, there may be internal damage in the form of concussion or compression.

Concussion may result in unconsciousness, shallow breathing, clammy skin and a rapid and weak pulse rate. Recovery to consciousness may be accompanied by nausea and vomiting. Compression is actual pressure on some part of the brain, by blood or fluid within the skull or by a depressed fracture of the skull itself. This condition may directly follow concussion with no return to consciousness, or it may develop a few hours after apparent recovery. The following symptoms may be present but the absence of any does not rule out compression.

- Unconsciousness and a coma may be evident from the outset, particularly if damage has occurred to the brain tissue.
- Irritation of the brain in the early stages may cause twitching of the person's limbs, or even convulsions.
- The body temperature may rise and the pulse rate become slow.
- The breathing may become rather noisy.
- The pupils of the eyes will tend to be abnormal and may become dilated, unequal in size or will not react to light.
- Weakness or paralysis on one side of the body may be evident.

In an unconscious person it is important to make sure that the breathing passages are not obstructed. False teeth or teeth knocked out by the accident should be carefully removed, preferably using a handkerchief. Clothing should be loosened about the neck, chest and waist. Ensure that the circulation of air around the casualty is not restricted, and place them in the recovery position (see Fig. 9.1) with the head slightly lower than the feet, so allowing secretions or vomit to drain away. The casualty should be kept warm and not left unattended if possible.

Severe shock

This arises from lack of blood supply and circulation and is associated with a number of physical conditions and injuries. It may be caused by a severe loss of body fluid or by psychological stress. Shock can usually be recognised by:

- faintness and giddiness;
- vomiting;
- cold and clammy skin with considerable sweating;
- consciousness may be clouded;

- an increase in pulse rate, which also tends to become weak;
- shallow and rapid breathing.

The casualty should be laid down, with clothing loosened around the neck, chest and waist, then covered as much as possible to keep them warm. If they are injured, do not move them more than necessary. Pressure should be applied to any bleeding points.

When a person faints it is usually because of a reduction in the blood supply to the brain, frequently caused by some emotional or sensory stimulus. It may begin by just a feeling of faintness, or it may show itself in a sudden collapse of the casualty. If a person is feeling faint, get them to breathe deeply and flex the muscles of the thighs, buttocks and legs to assist the circulation. It would also be advisable to loosen clothing around the neck, chest and waist. The casualty should either be laid down or should place the head between the knees until feeling better. If a person has already fainted, lay them down with the legs slightly above the level of the head, and clothing loosened around the neck, chest and waist. If breathing becomes difficult, place them in the recovery position (Fig. 9.1). When they regain consciousness raise them to a sitting position.

Burns

The seriousness of any burn depends largely on the area and extent affected.

If a passenger's clothes are on fire it may be possible to quench the flames with the aircraft fire extinguisher, but only an extinguisher filled with a dry chemical should be used and care must be taken not to direct the powder in the person's face.

If a suitable extinguisher is not available, approach the casualty holding a coat or other suitable material in front of you for protection. Wrap the coat around the casualty, who should be laid flat, then smother the fire by excluding the air. Do not use nylon or similar materials as they are themselves highly inflammable. If a person's clothing catches fire with no assistance available, he or she should immediately roll themselves on the ground to smother the flames.

When the fire is out remove anything restrictive in the vicinity of the burn before the damaged parts begin to swell. The casualty should be laid down. It is advisable not to remove burned clothing from burnt skin as it will probably do more damage and the clothing will most likely have been sterilised anyway by the heat. Copious amounts of cold water should be applied to the burn for as long as 15 minutes. The cooling effect will prevent further tissue damage resulting from endogenous (produced from within) heat production.

First aid kits

First aid kits which have to be carried by aircraft flying for public transport or aerial work, do not have to be approved by the Civil Aviation Authority, so pilots may come up against first aid kits with varying contents.

Although first aid kits are not a requirement for aircraft operating in the Private Category Certificates of Airworthiness, it is obviously advisable for them to be carried in any aircraft. They should include:

'First aid equipment of good quality, sufficient in quantity, having regard to the number of persons on board the aircraft, and including the following:

- roller bandages, triangular bandages, adhesive plaster, absorbent gauze, cotton wool (or wound dressings in place of the absorbent gauze and cotton wool), burn dressings, safety pins;
- haemostatic bandages or tourniquets, scissors;
- antiseptic, analgesic and stimulant drugs;
- a handbook on first aid'.

A first aid kit should be securely stowed in a convenient and easily accessible position and its contents should be checked at regular intervals.

Remember the basic	A – airway
	B – bleeding
	C – circulation
This could be life-saving.	

Part 2

Basic Aviation Psychology

IN AVIATION, A BASIC KNOWLEDGE OF
HUMAN PERFORMANCE AND
LIMITATIONS IS ESSENTIAL FOR THE
DEVELOPMENT OF JUDGEMENT AND
COMPETENCE IN DECISION MAKING

Chapter 10

The Human Information Process

The human information process basically starts with the physical senses, from which signals are transmitted via neural pathways to the brain. Here the information is interpreted, enabling the pilot to take the necessary physical actions.

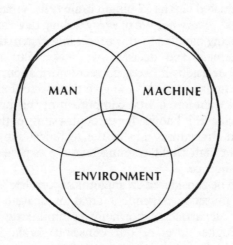

For this process to work correctly and efficiently, the signals from various senses should not conflict and the memory in the brain must hold knowledge to facilitate interpretation of the signals it receives. There are however potential weak links in the process and its resulting influence on a person's physical and psychological behaviour. On occasions any one of the senses can transmit misleading information, for example a visual image may give rise to an illusion, or the vestibular system in the inner ear may transmit signals which indicate that the aircraft is turning when in reality it is maintaining a straight path. The more we learn about false impressions, the more easily the brain will be able to untangle erroneous messages.

This leads us to the need for knowledge – gained by past study and experience, stored in the memory and brought into use as and when needed. Adequate knowledge is essential for the human information process to work correctly, and as far as pilots are concerned this cannot be over-emphasised.

It all starts with the master controller, the brain, which consists of a convoluted mass of nervous tissue contained in the skull. It controls sensation, learning and memory. It is just 3 lb in weight (1.36 kg) and is housed in a 6 × 8 in vault in the skull. The brain, which has been likened to a giant telephone exchange or a computer, handles incoming and outgoing calls and makes decisions as diverse as whether to laugh or cry, and whether to go round again or turn back or otherwise divert if the weather deteriorates. A computer of the same capacity as the brain would require a very large building in which to house it.

However, for the brain to react to any situation it needs information; in acting on this information it makes decisions and issues instructions. It receives the information from the sensory system and the memory store. This is then evaluated via the 12 billion brain cells, sometimes referred to as the 'think tank'. Every minute of every waking day a stream of unsifted information is being handled by this processing system that is responsible for every judgement and decision we make. But to make correct judgements and decisions it needs correct information, so as to evaluate the specific 'in flight situations' and give the correct instructions.

Knowledge is therefore a vital component of this processing system. The pilot has to gain this knowledge through a study of the aviation Rules, Regulations and Procedures and of the technical subjects of the pilot syllabus, and through flight training and the experience gained after qualifying for a licence.

The brain can be considered an anatomical correlate of the mind and is organised into mutually dependent areas of delegated responsibility. These areas or departments normally communicate freely with one another. The higher level of our conscious brain function can be compared with the top level management of a company; it is not bothered with small details but is merely concerned with policy or the declaration of objectives. The implementation of policy is handled by the lower, largely subconscious departments.

However, for the brain to function properly it needs stimulus, and in flying is heavily dependent on the sensory system. It is important to appreciate that our sensory organs are not able to detect all the information important to flight. For example, although acceleration and deceleration can be sensed through the receptors in our muscles and the balance mechanism of the inner ear, a pilot is unable to sense the actual speed of travel.

The important message from all this is that although human beings are equipped with a number of physical systems which supply the brain with information, these systems and the way they transmit signals to the brain can mean that mis-information is provided which may lead to the pilot making errors.

A further point of interest is that some sensory systems operate within a limited range, e.g. sounds of sufficiently high pitch cannot be detected by the human ear, and certain objects, due to the light frequency or conditions of light, may not be discernible to the human eye. In addition, individual sensory systems can be more sensitive in one person than another, and are also subject to deterioration with age, physical condition and the effects of certain drugs.

Concepts of sensation

Bodily sensations spring from the senses: sight, hearing, smell, touch and taste; in addition, and particularly during flight, the sense of balance derived from the inner ear mechanism is important.

These senses are highly developed in most individuals. For example touch, where the nerve endings in the fingers are sufficiently sensitive to detect whether we have turned over one or two pages of a newspaper, and the thickness of a sheet of newspaper is virtually negligible.

On the other hand, if the message sent to the brain from a pilot's muscles and joints (proprioceptive sense) conflicts with that received from the vestibular organ in the inner ear, the brain may be thrown into confusion, possibly resulting in inappropriate reactions which could have disastrous consequences. This is why pilots are taught to develop greater confidence in their sense of sight, and to believe the flight instruments when conditions dictate their sole use, such as in IMC or at night.

When the interpretation of senses by the brain, and communication within the brain, results in erroneous actions it can simply cause a person to tangle words, e.g. 'slips of the tongue' or a mix-up of physical actions such as looking for reading glasses when they are already being worn. In a pilot, it can cause the mixing up of numerals and setting the wrong QNH, or turning on to the wrong heading.

Bear in mind that there are no pilots who have not at some time reached out for the wrong knob, switch or lever, or having selected the right one, turned it the wrong way. This illustrates how faulty communication between areas of the brain, probably due to preoccupation with other matters, can result in erroneous actions which may lead to accidents.

Examples of accidents

The following two summaries relate to actual accidents and demonstrate the need to know one's own weaknesses, and develop the ability to concentrate on one thing at a time when operating aircraft systems.

(1) When a crashed aircraft was removed from a river, the mixture control was in the 'idle cut-off' position. The pilot stated that he closed the throttle and thought he applied full carburettor heat. When the engine seemed to be idling too slowly the throttle was advanced but the engine did not respond. The pilot assumed a fuel tank was empty and hurriedly switched tanks. Since this did not solve the problem, an emergency landing was attempted on the river bank.

(2) A business executive accompanied by two passengers departed on a business trip in a single engine aircraft. Soon after take-off the pilot experienced complete power failure, and the aircraft was landed straight ahead outside the airport. Investigation revealed the mixture control positioned three-quarters of the way to 'full lean'. The pilot stated that he was monitoring the tachometer and manifold pressure gauge and did not notice which control he used to change the propeller pitch!

Pilots should visually check a control prior to operating it, but this is not always practised. During take-offs and landings many pilots manipulate controls by touch while monitoring other traffic, communicating with the tower, or scanning instruments. When pilots are not looking at which knob, lever, switch or handle their hands are touching, the stage is set for a pilot-induced emergency. This is especially true when the pilot's attention is diverted by some unusual circumstances or outside distraction.

Perception

A pilot's physical actions are a direct response to what he or she perceives at the time. This perception is derived from the visual system, the motion sensing systems of the inner ear, and the position sensing system involving nerve endings in the skin, muscles and joints. All these systems are continually playing their part in telling the pilot what is happening, enabling a mental model to be formed, and from experience the pilot knows what to do in response. Thus pilots have to be physically fit so that their sensory systems are in good working order.

It is also a fact that most pilots, like other people, know when they are one degree under physically, and so know when not to fly . . . or do they? It is here that human factors play such a vital part in aviation safety.

Expectancy

Information from the sensory system is passed via the communications channels (the nerves) to the brain, which then sorts out the meaning of the message it receives. This is perception. However, if our expectancy or anticipation is sufficiently strong we may draw a wrong conclusion and the influences of expectancy (often called 'set') can have a powerful bearing on what we perceive and as a result we can make incorrect conclusions or responses.

A quick glance at Fig. 10.1 (a) followed by a careful reading of the words is a good example of how expectancy can lead to errors in what we perceive. Fig. 10.1 (b) illustrates another type of misperception: although the left horizontal line looks shorter than the one on the right, they are actually both the same length. (You will need to measure the lines to prove this.) From these two simple examples you will see how easily misperceptions can occur.

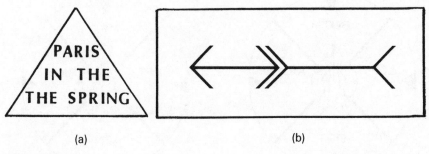

(a)   (b)

Fig. 10.1

During flight this can mean navigational errors, often politely referred to as 'geographic disorientation'. This simply means that the pilot has mis-identified a ground feature and so come to the wrong conclusion on where he is. This is often due to anticipation causing a mismatch between the familiar 'model' of what the pilot expects to see, and the actual position of the aircraft. In psychological terminology, this is called 'cognitive dissonance', i.e. a discrepancy between what a person expects to see and what he or she is actually seeing, or expressed in a wider context it means a lack of awareness that there is an absence of consistency.

The reader's reaction to that may be 'Well I do not navigate on an expectancy basis'. Sadly, however, only perfect humans can totally avoid expectancy. The rest of us will lapse into it from time to time, and the cockpit during flight is an ideal breeding ground for expectation.

Remembering this human trait will help your navigational ability, and will help you avoid landing at the wrong aerodrome – a situation which has happened to a number of pilots regardless of their experience or type of licence held.

Habits

Habits can also cause problems, as a large number of procedures and actions become automatic responses, although they may not be applicable to another similar type of operation or aircraft. For example, consider the many variations of fuel selector positions in different aircraft. If a pilot regularly flies a specific aircraft, the movement of the fuel selector to the on, off, or appropriate tank can become an automatic action (motor memory). Fig. 10.2 shows the fuel selector layout of two currently used light aircraft; note that the selector position for BOTH in (a) is the same as the OFF position in (b). So a habitual response could cause the fuel to be turned off.

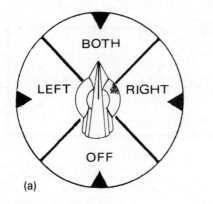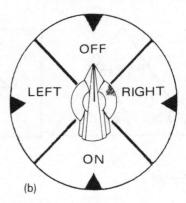

(a) (b)

Fig. 10.2 Fuel selectors

Such an error (behavioural reversion) may not be apparent imme-diately because when the fuel selector is turned off, the engine continues running for a short time while the fuel in the lines is used up. So a mis-selection during the pre-landing checks could lead to a serious accident.

In many instances, a pilot's actions are influenced by motivation, for example a pilot in a test is highly motivated to do things correctly. But in other circumstances, such as when a pilot is very relaxed, emotionally disturbed, fatigued or under high stress, the chances of errors due to expectancy or habitual actions are increased.

Cognitive perception

'Cognitive' covers the mental process of making judgements and decisions based on knowledge and awareness. Such knowledge and awareness is acquired by perception, reasoning or intuition. Perception is a conclusion reached about the nature and meaning of a message received through the senses; it is in effect an interpretive activity conducted through the process of information gathering.

The cognitive ability needed by a pilot could be simply expressed as the ability to put it all together and make the right decision at the right time. It should be appreciated that the ability to learn flying skills and memorise knowledge is no measure of a competent and safe pilot. The first of these only allows the pilot to enter a more risky environment – the air. The second will only be of value if the knowledge gained is put to good use, i.e. to come to a good decision. It is a fact that many pilots of undoubted skill have lost their lives by getting into situations where skill or aircraft performance could not extricate them, and many pilots who gained first class examination results have gone the same way. So, although skill and knowledge are both necessary, alone they will not create a safe pilot. The ingredient which must be added is the ability to make good judgements and correct decisions.

It is to achieve this that the subject of human performance and limitations has been introduced into the training of pilots. Thus this section of this manual is aimed at leading you to a practical understanding of judgement and decision making, drawing together the knowledge from Part 1 and the training received from your flying instructors.

Central decision channel

While one aspect of the human information process results in the storage of information in the memory, another aspect relates to the making of judgements and decisions. It should be borne in mind that humans effectively have only one decision channel and can only make one decision at a time. On the other hand, all the information from our various sensors is passing simultaneously into the central decision channel, and in effect this is like listening in on a multi-party shared telephone line in which several people are speaking at the same time.

To a pilot this is the same as visual, physical and aural perceptions, such as height and distance from the runway, bodily sensations, interaction with air traffic control, monitoring the attitude of the aircraft, reading the instruments, etc. All these inputs are sharing the central decision channel so information is being passed back and forth between the decision making source and the various memory stores of the brain.

Many people feel they can make several decisions at the same time, but they cannot; it simply seems like it because many motor responses are completely automatic and rapidly implemented. For example, when a typist is at work the decision to hit the correct key is a totally automatic response, based on practice and experience. You have only to sign your name and your pen will probably have moved in thirty directions or more in the space of two or three seconds, yet the only decision was to produce your signature; the rest was totally automatic.

In the making of non-automated decisions, however, a period of concentration is necessary; it may be short or long, depending on the factors involved in weighing up the situation and arriving at a decision.

Limitations of mental workload

If too many pieces of information or ambiguous items enter the decision channel it can easily become overloaded, leading to important information being ignored. In addition, if high stress levels are involved a person may concentrate on one input and ignore the others. Either of these could easily lead to faulty judgements or decisions.

An awareness of these factors will help you to appreciate that we all have certain limitations. These not only vary from individual to individual but also within ourselves depending on the situation at the time.

Attention, information sources and stimuli

In general a person's attention is gained by a stimulus, usually derived from an information source. This source can be physical, e.g. the sound of a stall warner, or psychological, e.g. a thought which occurs in the mind and which drives the information process in the brain to concentrate on a particular aspect.

A person can also be limited in any stimulus situation, in that it is not normally possible to listen coherently to two people talking at the same time. Instructors tend not to appreciate this when talking to a student during flight. If there is an RTF transmission going on at the same time as the instructor is speaking, the student will be distracted. Although we have two ears, it is not easy to listen to two messages at the same time and make sense of them, so vital information may not be received by the student. The instructor might then think he has a poor student, whereas a reasonably intelligent student knows that he has an inconsiderate instructor! During training either the radio volume must be kept very low, or the instructor should pause to allow completion of the RTF message before speaking.

The environment of the aircraft cockpit or flight deck can often interfere with the ability to give attention to a specific item. On the one hand, the structure of the aircraft tends to inhibit lookout from the cockpit windows, and on the other, due to the frequency of audio communications, there will often be distractions between seeing and hearing. Added to this, there are many items which have to be monitored on a fairly continuous basis, such as flight, engine and system instruments, as well as charts, flight logs etc.

Therefore a safe pilot has to put great effort into achieving a method of paying selective attention to information received – one which is capable of avoiding distracting stimuli but alert to changing attention priorities when needed. This, however, is a difficult task as people are limited in their ability to perceive signals which occur simultaneously from more than one sensory source.

A particularly relevant example occurred in a controlled environment. Following an accident to a Boeing 737 at Manchester airport, when the aircraft caught fire during the take-off run with the loss of many lives, the UK Civil Aviation Authority commissioned a project to evaluate evacuation procedures of public transport aircraft. One of the aims was to find out why some survivors who were seated a long way from the exits were able to evacuate, while others sitting next to exits were not.

In the project, three separate evacuations were conducted. In each case the same volunteers were used, and a financial reward was promised to the first people to get out of the aircraft. One healthy, strong male succeeded in being in the first group to get out on the first two occasions. However, on the third evacuation he realised that because his seat was so far away from the nearest door there was no point in trying to make a rapid exit, because his chances of financial reward were virtually nil.

On leaving the aircraft with the tail enders, he asked the controller of the evacuation why, on this last occasion, a tape recorded sound-track had been played which emitted screams and other noises. The controller informed him that the sound track had been used during every evacuation.

The message from this is clear. The healthy strong male had been so absorbed and determined to earn his additional financial reward on the first two evacuations, that he had been totally unaware of the sound-track being played.

This type of total attention can be related to other types of inherent accident situations. Although aural or visual stall warnings are fitted in most aircraft, the pilot's attention must be highly distracted for them to actuate, otherwise he or she would have been monitoring the airspeed indicator and the impending stall situation would not have occurred.

Distracting influences can thus cause dangerous situations, and neither the aural noise nor the visual light may be able to break through the pilot's 'attention set'. Therefore total reliance on such warnings is misplaced. Statistics show this to be the case. In early aircraft such warning indicators did not exist and a significant number of aircraft inadvertently stalled or spun. Today, when the majority of aircraft are fitted with stall warning devices, they continue to stall and spin with the same regularity as before.

While there are other factors to be considered, the inescapable conclusion is that these devices are not very effective at preventing stall/spin accidents.

Verbal communication

One of the vital information sources is verbal communication – the life-blood of aviation activity when more than one person is involved. However, such a method of communication is prone to errors involving anticipation, expectation, errors in speech, or distortion of the transmission. All or any of these can occur during information transfer by radio telephony, when speaking too fast, clipping transmissions, using incorrect phraseology, or the presence of background noise can all interfere with the quality of transmission/reception.

Pilots must constantly be on their guard against all of these. RTF transmissions spoken too rapidly can defeat the speed at which intelligent perception can work, and can result in guesswork. Clipped transmissions can lead to the same problem, and together with incorrect phraseology and background noise, (poor signal to noise ratio) can lead to pilots believing they have heard what they anticipated.

These types of erroneous communication have in the past led to a number of accidents. Pilots must remain conscious of these errors, whenever communicating verbally, and must not be afraid to request 'say again' whenever they have the slightest doubt about the message. Standard words and phrases have been laid down for radio telephony transmissions, but flightcrew and air-traffic controllers alike should beware of jumping to conclusions, and must double check whenever the slightest doubt arises in the quality of the message or its meaning.

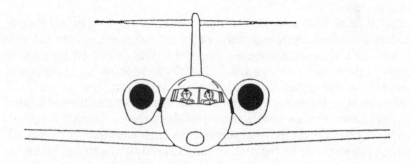

"Did you say 'take off power' or 'take-off power'?"

Memory

Memory symbolises the mental faculty of retaining and recalling knowledge and past experiences. However, like so many human functions, memory occurs in varying degrees and the level of recall varies between different people and also the same person from day to day.

The ability to store and retrieve knowledge is essential to the normal functions of our daily lives, and when operating an aircraft it becomes vital to safety. Thus a greater understanding of how our memory works and how it is affected by our physical and mental condition, can lead to a better performance in aviation activities.

Memory is the ability of the brain to register information, store it, associate it with previous information and recall it when needed. Every perception we derive, such as sensation, emotions or ideas, is processed within the brain. This main portion of the central nervous system is made up of billions of connecting cells, and it is the number of these linkages and the information they carry that give us our memory power.

The same item of memory may be stored in a number of different brain cells and the number we use at any one time will vary. This explains why brain cells can be lost through age or damage, yet a person can still have clear memories of a large number of past experiences.

Types of memory

In a simple way, the human information processing system can be considered as having three different stores of information from which recall is made. These are known as the short term memory, the long term memory and the working memory.

The expression 'short term memory' refers to information which is stored for a very short time and then forgotten. It is usually limited to a

Short term memory

Long term memory

Working memory

few items of information for a few seconds. An example of this would be the reading of a telephone number and then, due to a lack of recall, having to read it again before completing the dialling sequence. Figure 10.3 shows the approximate memory retention of our short term recall ability.

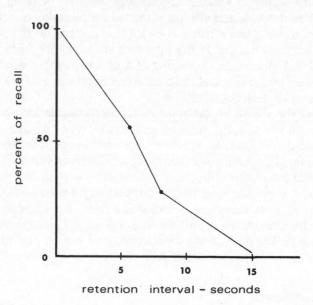

Fig. 10.3

Long term memory, as the expression indicates, represents the facility to recall information which has been stored either by repetition and constant recall, or by a vivid occurrence. It is information which is not currently being used but is held in a 'warehouse' which has an enormous capacity to store all accumulated knowledge. Nevertheless, as we have all found out from time to time, our long term memory does have certain retrieval problems and Figure 10.4 shows our approximate ability to remember items against the number of recalls actually made.

One method of improving recall is known as 'overlearning'. It means carrying the training process beyond that required to perform an acceptable standard of performance. This concept, built into any training programme, helps recall and also strengthens resistance to stress as well as improving psychomotor tasks.

Another aspect of memory is that continuous recall of specific items, or conducting motor tasks with a good level of continuity, enhances the ability to remember or carry out tasks. This is known as 'continuous activity'. On the other hand, tasks which require separate responses (serial tasks), are more easily forgotten.

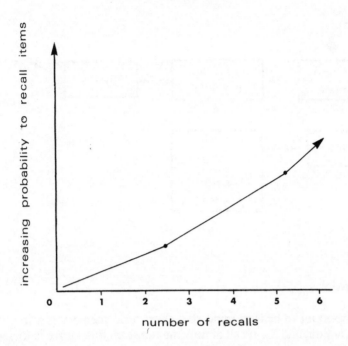

Fig. 10.4

The expression 'working memory' is used to indicate information we are currently using. For example, when reading from a checklist our working memory is using information from both our short and long term memory stores, to translate the meanings of the words into the necessary cognitive and physical activities, such as whether or not we would use flap for take-off, or to calculate, for instance, whether there is sufficient fuel on board to safely complete the flight.

Although our short term memory is normally restricted to recalling six to eight items, it can be improved by 'chunking'. This is a method of taking unrelated letters and associating them with familiar words so we can remember the words, and if we extend the words into sentences many more words can be remembered. In a sense this is similar to the use of those fairly common mnemonics such as FREDA or HASELL which are introduced from the early stages of pilot training. The use of chunking is therefore a valuable asset to our working memory.

An illustration of how the types of memory fit into the chain of sensory perceptions, memory function and ultimate response is shown in Figure 10.5.

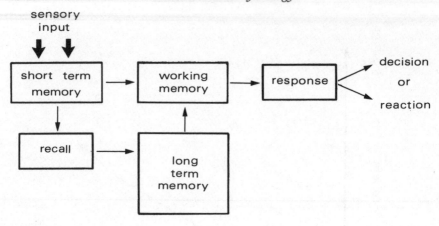

Fig. 10.5

Limitations

It is important to bear in mind that short term memory is a frequently used function, and the recall of information from this source is somewhat fleeting.

The information it imparts to our working memory is prone to error, and pilots must be aware that transient information quickly accepted, and often of a length which cannot accurately be held in the short term memory, has been the cause of many mistakes in the past.

A typical example of memory limitation is when air traffic controllers who are under pressure pass information quickly, and often in a single transmission, which can defeat the short term memory recall of a pilot. This is a particular problem when a pilot is under a high workload.

The result of this on many occasions has been the misunderstanding of information on cleared altitudes, flight levels, pressure settings, etc. In multi-crew operations this type of error is reduced by one crew member monitoring the other. However, in single pilot operations the errors can be reduced only by not hesitating to request 'say again' when necessary, and by the use of the 'double check' procedure after commencing or completing the response to the message received.

Another important aspect which can affect the accuracy of the information we store in our short term memory is the degree of expectancy, i.e. what we expect to hear or see. This can sometimes be strong enough to replace what we have actually heard or observed. In summary, it should be appreciated that there will always be the danger of assuming we are perceiving what we want to perceive, rather than sending a true message to our short term or working memory.

Stress

Causes and effects

In everyday language the word stress implies a nervous strain or mental tension. In aviation 'pilot stress' can become a complex and sometimes misused term. When flying an aircraft, the pilot is in control of certain forces which apply stress to the airframe and power plant. If the pilot operates the controls in such a manner that the aircraft exceeds the design load factor, certain components can be weakened, or in serious overload fracture or total failure can be caused.

Thus, during their training, pilots become aware of how the aircraft they fly responds to stress. To operate safely and efficiently a pilot also needs to know how the human body responds to physical and mental stresses. Whereas the response to physical stress may be fairly easily recognised, the responses we make to mental stress can be insidious.

Perhaps the simplest way to understand human stress is to relate it to the material strength of an aircraft. The demands placed on it by the pilot or the environment in which it flies, must not exceed its capacity to meet them.

overstressed

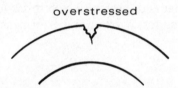

In relation to the human body too, this is what stress is all about. Overstress could be defined as placing demands upon ourselves which exceed our capacity to cope with them. This means that whenever demands go above a certain level – or alternatively when our resources go down i.e. feeling unwell or already under pressure – we are in danger of becoming overstressed, with a resulting deterioration in our ability to cope.

There are of course other definitions of stress, which more or less mean the same, for example:

... the body's non-specific response to demands placed upon it, whether these demands are pleasant or unpleasant.

... an unresolved pressure, strain or force acting upon the pilot's mental and physical systems which, if continued, will cause damage to those systems.

Continued stress can create physical symptoms such as insomnia, loss of appetite, headaches, irritability, etc. The stimulus for stress is known as the stressor, which is the force producing a change in the self-regulating balance between a human's internal and external environment. This stimulus will demand a response which may be psychological or physiological. Thus we see that the stressor is the stimulus, and the stress is the response to it.

Concepts of arousal

Before discussing the management and avoidance of stress, it must be appreciated that it is an inescapable part of human life. In other words, it is impossible to live without experiencing some degrees of stress, whether at home, during our working role or at leisure. Further, an optimum amount of stress is needed for us to function efficiently in flying operations.

This can best be explained by a person's state of arousal, which is a convenient way of demonstrating a person's preparedness for a difficult task. It has been suggested that arousal and performance are related by an inverted U-shaped curve (known as the Yerkes–Dodson curve) as shown in Figure 10.6. Deep sleep forms one end of the arousal axis, with sheer panic forming the other end, both of which result in poor performance. The optimum arousal for maximum performance is somewhere in between.

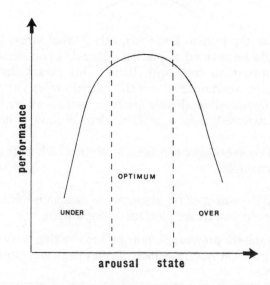

Fig. 10.6

By studying Figure 10.6 it can be seen that an optimum arousal factor produces an optimum performance. However, if we are bored, complacent or under aroused, as occurs in fatigue, or over aroused such as when mental or physical pressures are high, our performance will deteriorate.

Professors Ashman and Telfer of the Universities of Queensland and Newcastle (Australia) described stress and the way our bodies react to it in their Training Manual on Pilot Judgement, based on work by Selye:

'What is Stress?

Stress is the term we used to describe how the body reacts to demands placed upon it. Regardless of whether the demands are pleasant or unpleasant, the body reacts in basically the same way to any change. The change for you could be an unexpected windsheer encountered on landing, or discovering a serious unserviceability of your aircraft during a pre-flight inspection immediately prior to an important business flight, or the backfiring of a car, or losing your wallet, or even travelling on vacation.

In any one of these, or similar events, our bodies will make a three stage response to such demands and in the following order:

(1) *Alarm reaction.*   In the alarm stage the body recognises the stress-producing event (called a stressor), and prepares for fight or flight by the release of hormones. These hormones increase heartbeat and rate of breathing, raise blood sugar level, increase perspiration, and slow digestion. Depending upon the recognition of danger, the process may result in a burst of energy, greater muscular strength, and even better hearing and vision.

You may have experienced several alarm reactions during your flying, perhaps when you encounter a sudden buffeting on late finals, or dealing with a difficult crosswind during landing.

(2) *Resistance.*   In the resistance stage, the body sets about repairing any damage caused by the stress, enabling it to adapt to some sustained stressors, such as extreme cold, hard physical labour, or worries. If the stress continues over a long period (as in VMC that deteriorate to IMC or an increasingly obvious fuel shortage), the body will try to maintain its arousal state of readiness.

(3) *Exhaustion.*   Exhaustion is generally temporary and affects only specific parts of the body. For instance, marathon runners experience severe stress in their muscles and cardiovascular system, leading to exhaustion, and pilots who fly for very long periods can experience exhaustion when they go off duty. However, after a good rest, they are looking forward to the next race or flight. If the combination of resistance and exhaustion continues without relief over a long period,

there may be a risk of disease (such as high blood pressure, migraine headaches, stomach upsets, or asthma). The body may even give up completely, resulting in death.'

As already mentioned, it is impossible to live without experiencing some degree of stress, and life without occasional stress would be pretty dull. In reasonable doses stress adds to the excitement of life. Several types of stressors are pleasurable, such as the exhilaration we feel as we accelerate down the runway on take-off. A certain amount of stress is needed for well-being and to enable us to achieve peak performances for important jobs. For example, we hear of people performing amazing feats of strength in emergency situations.

Other stressors can cause us to miss important information and make errors of judgement. If this type of stress occurs during a flight, it can threaten our lives.

Stressors

Most of the stressors we encounter are emotional, but the impact of them depends more on how we react to the stress than on what caused it. Unfortunately it is very easy for us to dismiss the effect of stress, especially when we think that it has little effect on us. In pilot judgement training, we are not only concerned with stress that occurs during flight but also with the stress that pilots bring to the aircraft as a result of problems at work or family and life pressures. We are interested in these because stress is cumulative, i.e. it builds up like water being added to a bucket until it overflows. Pilot judgement training advocates punching a hole in the bucket to ensure that the overflow never occurs.

The total stress which can be imposed on a pilot can be divided into three sources:

(1) *Environmental stressors (physical)* These are related to the normal events which occur during a pilot's flying activities.
(2) *Life stressors (psychological)* These include emotional, domestic, social and financial causes.
(3) *Reactive stressors* These are the body's physical or mental response to certain situations which arise in everyday life, as well as those which arise when operating an aircraft.

Environmental stressors
These can occur singly or collectively, and are created by noise, vibration, heat, lack of oxygen, presence of carbon monoxides and the onset of fatigue, etc. Others are directly related to the tasks involved in flying and

the degree of stress will vary from flight to flight. Provided good weather prevails, the planning and accomplishment of a flight along a route that the pilot has done many times before, will result in minimal stress. However, if a new route is to be flown and/or the weather condition could produce problems, the stress may be fairly high.

Similarly, the stress imposed on a pilot can vary with the flight phase, for example, en route flying in good weather conditions will produce minimal stress, but during the approach to landing in difficult cross wind conditions stress will be much higher.

Life stressors

These are associated with events in our everyday lives. They are wide ranging and include such factors as domestic and financial problems which most of us face on a recurring basis. Family arguments, death of a close relative, inability to pay our bills, our life-style and personal activities, smoking or drinking to excess and other factors which may affect our physical and mental health, all come together in the amount of life stress which can be part of our everyday lives. All can significantly add to the operational stressors which all pilots have to cope with in their flying activities.

Reactive stressors

These stem from the body's reaction to specific events. For example, in the case of a pilot they could emanate from the aircraft suddenly sinking on the approach as it flies into a downdraught near the ground, or from the aircraft suddenly starting to veer off the runway centre line during the landing roll out, or from a more serious emergency, such as engine failure.

A pilot who is already under a high degree of stress from job related tasks and/or life events, is clearly 'one degree under' and not in good shape to cope effectively with emergencies. Stress in our social or work roles is cumulative, and on reaching a particular level can lead to serious difficulties and consequences.

Stress overload

Everyone has a personal stress limit and if this is exceeded a 'stress overload' occurs which can result in an inability to handle even moderate workloads. This personal stress limit varies with different people, as it is affected by a person's physiological and psychological characteristics. For example, some people have the ability to 'switch off' and relax, thus reducing the effects of stressors. Others are not so well equipped and the stress level increases to an unacceptable degree. When this happens to pilots, air traffic controllers or others whose job is related to aircraft operations, it can only spell danger. This particularly applies to pilots, who once airborne cannot escape from the additional pressures that are part of flight, let alone an emergency situation.

Anxiety and its relationship to stress

The causes of anxiety are manifold and at times rather complex, but the relationship of anxiety to stress is fairly straightforward.

Anxiety creates worry, and in turn any form of worry can lead to stress. Most anxiety is produced by knowing that we have no control over specific events, or that we lack the 'know how' to handle such events.

Anxiety is particularly prevalent in people who, for one reason or another, are lacking in self confidence. In the case of pilots this can only be changed by becoming more knowledgeable or gaining greater proficiency in operating an aircraft. To achieve either of these more time has to be devoted to study and flight training.

Our attitudes and general mental state are as important as the serviceability of our aircraft. Any disturbing feelings which affect our ability to concentrate are a potential threat to safe flight. These feelings include fear, anger, frustration, worry, and anxiety, and these may also be a factor in the development of increased blood pressure (hypertension), which may be linked with heart disease. Thus long term mental pressure can have physical effects which could result in problems when obtaining or renewing a pilot's medical certificate.

To sum up, stress and anxiety are an inevitable part of human life and in small amounts they are also desirable. This is nature's way of keeping a person keyed up for a task; it helps concentration and makes recognition of danger easier. On the other hand excessive stress leads to excessive anxiety, just like other deep emotions which can cause a reduction in our ability to concentrate can lead to hazards in the cockpit.

Pilots who bring their ground problems into the cockpit will be more easily distracted and less able to adjust to various stresses. Memory, judgement and presence of mind are crucial during flight, and it is not always appreciated that muscular skills are closely related to mental capacity. For example, when a pilot becomes mentally disturbed or preoccupied, he or she will lose the ability to time physical movements accurately, or the brain may fail to interpret messages correctly from the sensory system.

If, as a pilot, you fly with family or job problems on your mind you may become preoccupied or develop fears about flying. If you fly following an argument, you may well find yourself recreating that argument in your mind, thinking about what you should have said. During thoughts of this nature you are more likely to make mistakes, e.g. forgetting to change fuel tanks or mis-selecting one of the aircraft systems. Mental pressures and anxieties are bad companions in the cockpit, so if you are under strain your best decision is to remain on the ground. When only mild everyday concerns are affecting you, then at least recognise that they exist and make an extra effort to focus your attention on the job in hand; when you leave the ground leave your other concerns behind, or you will not be in the right state of mind to fly safely.

These are not simple cures for the problem, because it will require positive effort coupled with sufficient time and finance before a pilot arrives at a confident state of mind for flying. Nevertheless, the gaining of greater knowledge and continual flying practice, particularly the handling of simulated emergencies, will go a long way to reducing anxiety, both before and during flight.

Effects of stress on human performance

The benefits of moderate stress in obtaining optimum performance have already been mentioned. Moderate stress causes an immediate reaction, in that the body prepares itself for a particular effort. This process can lead to an increase in energy, better hearing, quicker reactions and greater muscular strength.

If stress is maintained the body may continue to adapt itself to cope with the prevailing circumstances, or alternatively it may reach a stage of exhaustion. This can lead to poor judgement and decision making, and if there is no relief a number of stress induced illnesses can develop, to a life threatening extent.

Bear in mind that the effects of physiological and psychological stressors are cumulative, and herein lies the greatest danger to the pilot. Furthermore stress can sometimes be insidious, in that a person could be suffering moderate stress due to social or emotional pressures and at this point may be able to cope with the situation. However, on entering the cockpit further stresses of a moderate nature are inevitably felt, and in these circumstances a pilot could find that his ability to handle stress becomes overloaded.

An important aspect of stress overload, which has not been mentioned so far, is the involvement of 'time' and the way it affects our psychological stressors. The ingredients for 'time induced stress' are an integral part of our way of life and can become particularly acute during flight operations. Time, or rather the lack of it, is a factor which induces emotional stress and has featured in many aircraft accidents. The need to get to a certain place at a certain time has been the primary cause of many pilots pressing on into deteriorating weather, with fatal consequences. Stress brought about by lack of sufficient time induces particular mental states, such as feelings of desperation and sometimes helplessness. Pilots should appreciate how this can create a situation for making bad decisions. The ability to recognise the warning signs of pressures brought about by lack of time will help pilots avoid this kind of stress. Bear in mind that it is not the lack of time available, but rather a pilot's response to it, which can make the difference between good and bad decisions. Professors Telfer and Ashman, in their series of Pilot Judgement Manuals, give some good advice on this:

'... it is important for pilots to recognise the warning signs of racing against time so that they can avoid this source of stress. In this respect, there are several signs you should consider in order to avoid chronic overload:

Do you seem to be constantly in a rush? Eat on the run? Hate to wait in line or be inconvenienced? Never seem to catch up? Schedule more activities than you have time available? Drive too fast most of the time? Become impatient if others are too slow? Have little time for relaxation, intimacy, or enjoying your environment?

Most of us go back and forth between such hurried behaviour and a more relaxed schedule, but if you had to answer 'yes' to more than a couple of the questions above, you may be well on the way to chronic overload.

Some people can and do live 'in the fast lane' because their bodies and minds can handle a fast pace. Others learn to adjust to a fast pace. You can learn how to stay healthy while accepting a hectic lifestyle, but the chances of increasing stress to a damaging level become high, especially for people who are not aware of the dangers, or do little or nothing about them.'

Juggling time and events
This means attempting to cram several activities into insufficient time. The human brain seems to lack the capacity to perform efficiently many conscious operations at the same time. It is difficult to prevent one task from interfering with another. Too many pressures can lead to distress.

Overcommitment and self-imposed obligations
Many people are unable to say no to requests and this may lead to stress when they realise that commitments made cannot be met. Overcommitment also occurs when zealous people take on obligations knowing that the likelihood of completing them is remote. You will probably be

aware of situations in which self-imposed obligations have led to serious aviation accidents and death.

Much of our life stress comes from self-imposed obligations. Does yours? If so, you need to reduce these obligations.

Identifying and reducing stress

The first step in reducing stress is to recognise when you are approaching your normal stress limit; inevitably this is rather a personal evaluation. Although most pilots have had no formal training in psychology, they are still capable of assessing their emotional or physical condition to the extent of their degree of fitness to fly.

Pilots are responsible for determining their physical and emotional condition prior to each flight, and in general terms they are well able to assess when they are 'one degree under'. The problem lies in their response and attitude towards their self assessment, and this will usually be the weakest link in the chain of their command responsibility. In other words, there are a number of occasions when pilots climb into the cockpit knowing full well that their physical and emotional state tells them they should really remain on the ground.

This manual is not intended as a do-it-yourself psychologist kit, but aims at highlighting some essential pointers for assessing your personal stress limit. If you learn to recognise some of the warning signals which tell you that your stress levels are becoming too high, you will at least have given yourself the opportunity to take action.

Warning signals include emotional tension, a feeling of being 'uptight', irritability, dryness of the mouth and throat, the tendency to be easily startled by minor events or unexpected sounds, a depressed attitude and a lack of patience towards others. It could of course be argued that many of these could be present without necessarily being associated with stress levels. On the other hand their mere presence is a signal for you to consider your optimum performance level during flight. So either way, their presence or absence will be helpful when making the decision whether to fly.

Because humans vary widely in their physical and psychological make up, and because their life styles and environments also vary, it is not easy to give specific advice on how to reduce stress. Therefore this manual can only tackle stress reduction in general terms, and it is appropriate to consider this aspect in relation to:

• physical well-being;
• psychological state;
• job performance.

Physical well-being
Actions consistent with good health would be:

(1) Stop or moderate activities such as smoking or drinking alcohol to excess.
(2) Learn to relax at frequent intervals.
(3) Take physical exercise on a regular basis.
(4) Eat regularly; avoid missing meals.
(5) Take 'time out' occasionally and indulge in deep breathing exercises for short periods.
(6) If you drive, try to avoid peak traffic times; this is not easy, and if impossible and you get held up, avoid frustration by forcing yourself to relax; apply patience and indulge in a few deep breathing exercises. If you can, move your muscles to improve blood circulation and flexibility.
(7) Make positive attempts to regulate your time keeping. Rushing causes stress, and impulsive actions often lead to errors. Avoid getting steamed up if you are late. Do not allow unforeseen events to compound the situation.
(8) When faced by demanding tasks try to limit their duration; a few minutes break will lower your stress level and improve subsequent performance.

It will not always be possible to follow some of these guidance points, but that should not deter you from making a positive effort.

Psychological state
Your well-being and job performance will be affected by your mental condition. Pressures of work as well as domestic and other social problems all have a bearing on your mental attitude, and many of these can lead to worry, anxiety and loss of self confidence.

(1) Avoid taking yourself too seriously. Many people on occasions put pride before common sense and the need to be sociable with others.
(2) The development of a good sense of humour is an excellent way of avoiding emotional stress.
(3) People who are good companions rate as being sociably acceptable. It is much better to be gregarious than a loner. Companionship gives the opportunity to discuss one's worries and share experiences. This often becomes a relief valve and reduces the build up of unacceptable stress.
(4) Be positive and tackle your responsibilities and problems as they occur. Avoid the tendency to put things off in the hope that they will go away.

(5) Avoid wishful thinking or a tendency always to expect the worst.
(6) Take care not to over-commit yourself. Some people take on too many tasks, only to find they cannot be accomplished in time if at all. Situations of this nature are ideal breeding grounds for the development of stress.

Job performance
This involves reactive stressors which concern both physical ability and mental processes. It is during flight planning and flying that all stressors come into their own. Clear thinking, free from emotional or physical worries, becomes of paramount importance. Simple mistakes can lead to more disastrous consequences than most mistakes which occur in the home.

Accidents during flight often occur because the task requirements exceed the pilot's capabilities, and this is more likely to occur when the pilot brings his ground-borne stressors (emotional or physiological) into the cockpit.

Chapter 11

Judgement and Decision Making

On the subject of judgement, it would perhaps be helpful to examine first the modular concept in which good judgements and decisions have to be made. Figure 11.1 illustrates how the interface of flightcrew, machine, systems, equipment and software come together in the airspace environment. It is based on the modular conception developed by Professor Edwards in 1972 which has become known as the SHEL concept.

In Figure 11.1 S indicates the software – the procedures and rules which pilots have to follow, the checklists which have to be used, symbology, etc. H stands for the hardware – the aircraft, its systems and equipment. E is the environment in which the man/machine system operates. L is the liveware – the pilots who operate the aircraft and interact with other personnel.

The central function in the model is the flightcrew, who have to manage the other components in a manner which results in a safe flight. In other words, it is the human – the most flexible – component, which makes the judgements and decisions to bring all the factors into a harmonious and safe working whole.

However, the problems that humans can fall prey to when operating an aircraft are many, such as:

- Information transfer problems
  breakdown in communication between people, pilots and air traffic controllers;
  misunderstood radio messages;
  insufficient recall of the aircraft operating manual and ATC procedures.
- language difficulties when flying internationally;
- mis-read checklists;
- mis-interpreted instrument indications;
- incorrect operation of system controls;
- task saturation, which can cause the human mind to tune out and ignore vital information when the workload gets too great;

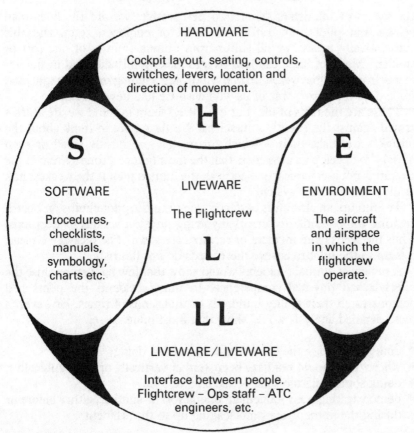

HARDWARE

Cockpit layout, seating, controls, switches, levers, location and direction of movement.

H

S

SOFTWARE

Procedures, checklists, manuals, symbology, charts etc.

LIVEWARE

The Flightcrew

L

E

ENVIRONMENT

The aircraft and airspace in which the flightcrew operate.

LL

LIVEWARE/LIVEWARE

Interface between people. Flightcrew – Ops staff – ATC engineers, etc.

Fig. 11.1

- weather deterioration;
- fatigue and subtle incapacitation;
- bad habits developed during training or afterwards;
- psychological problems which create other distracting situations, causing temporary or longer term errors.

Any of these and similar problems can create distractions or confusion which in turn cause deterioration in a pilot's judgement, cognitive process and psychomotor ability. So the SHEL model aptly describes the many influences affecting the pilot during flight.

Pilot judgement concepts

There is no panacea for incidents or accidents, but it will help us all if we get the most important point into perspective: we are firstly human beings, not pilots, air traffic personnel or engineers, etc., and this automatically means we all suffer from human frailties of one sort or another. Many of these can lead us into making mistakes and misjudgements from the time we get up in the morning to going to bed at night, and some days there are some of us who wish we had never got up.

These are the facts of life, but if we keep them in mind we are at least armed against the enemy – ourselves. We have only to think about the mistakes we make daily – which fortunately are mostly small or even trivial – to develop an awareness that the most failure-prone system in the aircraft is not mechanical or electrical; the human pilot is the weakest link in the man/machine system.

To sum up, an aircraft is perfectly safe until the pilot climbs on board, creating the potential for errors involving physical actions or decisions. Thus the seeds of an incident or accident are sown. The message is clear; it is up to the pilot to ensure these seeds do not flourish.

A review of annual accidents would show that few happen because the pilots lacked physical competence. In most accidents the pilots had demonstrated their ability hundreds or thousands of times. However, a more detailed analysis would show that most pilots were:

- doing something they should not have been doing;
- where they should not have been, (either vertically or geographically);
- doing something too soon or too late; or
- demonstrating poor judgement of one sort or another, either before or during the immediate events leading up to the accident.

However, pilots are not always to blame for the initial cause. A number of accidents have occurred due to serious power plant or systems failure, over which the pilot had no control. They have also occurred in circumstances which gave the pilot additional distractions when he or she was already coping with a high workload. In these situations the failure of the power plant or other system caused the pilot to fail to attend to other matters, which in turn led to a worsening situation and eventually an accident. Figure 11.2 shows how the relationship between human failures, machine failures and machine/human failures has changed over the years.

The pilot is often the victim of unnecessarily complex rules and procedures, thought up by people whose feet are firmly on the ground and who are divorced from the realities of the cockpit during flight. The introduction of large quantities of aviation legislation – much of which creates ambiguities or confusion in the mind of the pilot, particularly when performing multiple tasks under a collection of instructions, regulations and ATC procedures – can defy anyone but an aviation lawyer

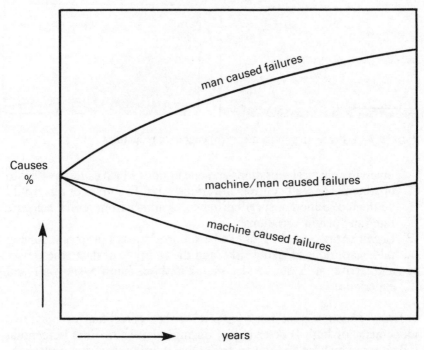

Fig. 11.2

to understand or remember, let alone abide by during critical phases of flight.

Thus accidents are usually the end result of a chain of events, and aircraft designers, manufacturers, mechanics, legislators or air traffic controllers cannot disassociate themselves completely from being a link in the chain.

Types of judgement

In general terms, judgement is a mental process by which pilots recognise, analyse and evaluate information about themselves, the aircraft and the operational environment. If good judgement is achieved, this will in turn lead to a timely and correct decision which will contribute to the safety of an aircraft.

Forming a judgement can be divided into two types, perceptive and cognitive (Fig. 11.3).

(1) *Perceptual judgement* Put simply this is a decision-making process

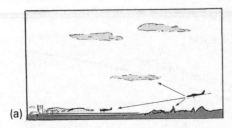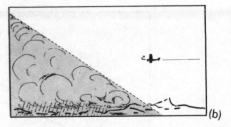

Fig. 11.3 (a) Perceptive judgement; (b) cognitive judgement

involving physical sensations and perceptions which cause the pilot to operate the aircraft controls in various ways. Examples of this would be the recognition of speed, distance, clearance from objects, closure rates and height variations.
(2) *Cognitive judgement*   This can be summed up as a process involving pilot's attitudes to taking risks, and the ability to evaluate these risks and arrive at a sound decision based on knowledge, skill and experience.

Every action a pilot takes involves either perceptual or cognitive judgement, or both. For example, during a level turn it is perceptual judgement which leads to the control of the aircraft's attitude in roll, bank, pitch, altitude and airspeed. The cognitive judgement lies in the decision to commence or continue the turn, and when to recover to straight and level flight. The need for situational awareness is paramount in all manoeuvres, and this involves the factors of time and lookout. Turning too early or too late, or failing to lookout prior to or during turning, are examples of poor cognitive judgement. Thus vigilant lookout is good judgement, which then becomes good airmanship.

Some examples of poor judgement would be:

• doing something which should not have been done;
• reacting too late or too early;
• doing too much or too little;
• doing nothing when something should have been done;
• trying to do too many things at the same time;
• allowing others less knowledgeable than you to dictate decisions.

There are of course many more, but the above examples give a clear indication of what should be avoided if one is to operate an aircraft sensibly and safely.

In the past, development of judgement was traditionally based on experience, skill and knowledge, with the ultimate quality of these measured under the collective term 'airmanship'. However, good airman-

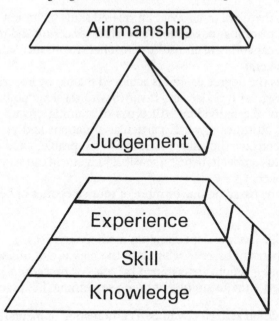

Fig. 11.4

ship can only be achieved through good judgement, which leads to the taking of a good decision. Thus the more logical arrangement of these factors would be: knowledge, skill, experience, judgement, airmanship (Fig. 11.4). In the training of pilots, these items should all be co-ordinated and developed together during each flight lesson.

Knowledge, skill and experience

These traditional aspects of pilot training form a natural combination, in that knowledge has to be gained before a skill can be developed and then improved by experience. In the past, pilot training at the *ab initio* stage has been based primarily on the development of perceptual and motor skills. A skill, as the word implies, is the capacity to accomplish successfully something requiring special knowledge or ability. The use of the words 'special knowledge or ability' implies that skills are not just related to physical activities, but to others such as social, intellectual, linguistic, etc.

In aviation, it is largely 'motor skills' which command most attention; this covers physical actions and the degrees of dexterity with which they are performed, i.e. with what precision the pilot handles the controls to make the aircraft adapt to the performance required.

However, there are other aviation related skills including competence in pre-flight planning, navigation, aircraft engineering and maintenance, as well as the capability of air traffic controllers to produce safe, regular air traffic movements.

In all cases the degree of skill is achieved mainly by experience, which stems from regular practice, and it varies with the adaptability and speed of learning of the individual. All types of training creates behavioural changes and attitudes towards particular situations and problems. It is essential to perceive the situation, identify the problem and consider the alternatives to combat it, before a sensible judgement can be arrived at and a decision taken.

This may be based on one or more of four categories of behaviour and competence:

(1) knowledge based – depending on memory and recall;
(2) comprehension based – relating to the measure of understanding;
(3) rule based – actions determined by rules or procedures;
(4) skill based – the technique of doing something, i.e. practical skill.

Thus the decision arrived at will be a combination of mental and physical functions which may be heavily affected by the constraint of time.

Cognitive judgement is the end result of perceiving a situation via the sensory system or memory. The hierarchical order of the brain then has to assess the situation and decide on a plan of action. In doing this, a pilot will be using knowledge gained from previous experience and will be evaluating the ability of the aircraft and himself to carry out the plan of action, or will consider whether an alternative plan is preferable.

In the implementation of knowledge, comprehension, rule or skill based functions, the brain is an error-detecting and error-correcting system. When subjected to misleading or insufficient information, it can also be an error-making system. Therefore the quality of our knowledge, skill and experience, together with our sensory and cognitive perception, plays a vital part in our sensible decision making.

Finally, in the development of aircraft handling skills, the term 'precognitive control' is sometimes used. This allows a pilot to achieve a higher performance level and occurs when the pilot knows what to do and is completely familiar with the aircraft handling characteristics. Continued practice enables a pilot to accomplish control movements so accurately timed and sequenced that they give very precise results.

Exercising judgement

The ability to exercise judgement is a unique capability of human beings. It enables them to evaluate data from numerous sources and as a result of training and experience to come to a conclusion. Judgement, however, may be seriously affected by psychological pressures such as stress, or by such human traits as personality, ego, temperament or other behavioural aspects. In addition, the lack of appropriate knowledge, or the inability to apply knowledge to the immediate situation, will certainly have an adverse bearing on the quality of judgement exercised.

Judgement training will initially relate to the following four factors:

(1) the pilot;
(2) the aircraft;
(3) time available;
(4) the environment.

Each of these basic elements contains risk factors which apply to every flight and to the reason for every flight. For example, some risks such as unexpected weather deterioration may be encountered during flight, while other risks such as a desire to get home may be involved even before the aircraft leaves the ground.

To apply good judgement, a developing hazard must be detected and the four factors must be reviewed. The pilot has to take action in order to reduce or eliminate any increase in risk. This action must then be monitored to ensure it is working as intended.

Poor judgement

In accident summaries published by those concerned with aviation safety, 'causal factors' are given, e.g. loss of control, power plant or other systems failure, pressed on into deteriorating weather, insufficient length of take-off or landing path, etc. However, it should be remembered that the factor identified as the cause of the accident is in many cases merely the end result of the initial causal factor, i.e. a demonstration of poor judgement and lack of correct decision making by the pilot.

When we read or hear of an aircraft accident due to bad weather, or one in which the aircraft failed to take-off or land safely within the available distance, it was so often not the weather or any deficiency in the length of the take-off or landing run available that caused the accident, but rather an earlier bad judgement or decision. The following two examples, taken verbatim from published accident summaries, illustrate this point.

'... The probable cause of the accident was that the pilot, who was relatively inexperienced and not qualified to engage in low level operations, allowed the aircraft to stall at a height too low for recovery to be effected.'

This accident was listed under causal factors as 'loss of control'. However, it does not take a great deal of intelligence to appreciate that the actual cause of the accident was the pilot's decision to engage in low flying, particularly in view of his limited flying experience. Thus the real causal factor was 'poor judgement' rather than loss of control.

The second example relates to a pilot who decided to practice an engine failure after take-off situation. The accident summary reads:

'. . . Following a practice engine failure after take-off, the pilot opened up to full power to climb away. After a few seconds the engine failed and the aircraft crashed into a wood.'

The causal factor given to this accident was 'engine failure', but was it? Here we have the classic scenario of a pilot practising to improve his competence – in case this type of emergency should occur – at low height immediately after take-off.

The fact that the pilot was practising for such an event proved that he was fully aware that such an emergency could happen. He was equally aware of the possibility that the engine could fail at a low height, while the aircraft was climbing away following the practice situation. Clearly this fact was not taken into account. If it had been the pilot, in the exercise of good judgement, would not have practised the procedure unless the climb away path was reasonably clear of obstructions, instead of over a large wood.

To sum up, the pilot deliberately placed himself in a situation where there was no escape route should the emergency for which he was practising actually occur. Therefore the real causal factor was simply bad judgement, rather than the fact that the engine failed at a most inappropriate moment. It is only by considering the relevant facts before making decisions, that good judgements can be made. This is what the development of good judgement and decision making is all about.

Examples of good and bad judgement

How the four factors of pilot, aircraft, time and the environment relate to each other in the exercise of judgement is illustrated in the following examples:

The pilot
Example 1: Before flight Following a very busy day with abnormal mental stress, the pilot slept badly. He had planned to take two friends on a 300 nm navigation flight and return the same day. However, on the morning of the intended flight the pilot, appreciating the effects of his sleepless night and the possible onset of fatigue during the flight, decided,

most sensibly, to postpone it to another day.

Conclusion   To have tackled the flight in these circumstances would have been a display of poor judgement.

Example 2: During flight   One of the passengers asked the pilot to take him to the area where he lived and circle his house which is in open countryside. The pilot responded to his passenger's wish and diverted from the planned route. Heavy rain showers were in the locality at the time, and the pilot increased speed to get to the passenger's house before an approaching rain shower moved into the area. The pilot then descended below his selected safety altitude so that his passenger would have a better view of his home.

At this stage, while circling his passenger's house, he flew into the rain shower, which reduced visibility significantly. The pilot had now placed himself and his passengers in a situation where at low height and in poor visibility, just one more factor, e.g. a malfunctioning power plant, would place them all in a risk situation which could have fatal consequences.

Conclusion   In this scenario we see what might have been a simple and relatively safe situation changing rapidly into a high risk encounter. Good judgement at an early stage would have made the pilot change his mind and return to his original flight plan, leaving the visit over his passenger's house for a more suitable occasion.

The aircraft
Example 3: Before flight   During the pre-flight inspection the pilot noticed that the fuel vent pipe had been damaged and he made a mental note to report it after the flight. Shortly after take-off the engine failed due to an inadequate fuel flow as a result of the damaged fuel vent opening.

Conclusion   Good judgement demanded that an engineer be called to rectify the damage to the fuel vent before the aircraft was flown.

Example 4: During flight   Following a visual check of the fuel tank contents prior to the flight, the pilot of a high wing aircraft noticed that en route the fuel gauges lowered much more quickly than usual. He put this down to inaccurate fuel contents gauges and continued towards his destination. Two hours short of his calculated endurance, the engine failed while the aircraft was over water.

The true cause of the unusual consumption indication was that a fuel cap had been improperly secured, which led to fuel venting due to low pressure over the wings.

Conclusion   On noting the apparent high rate of fuel being used, good judgement demanded that the pilot should divert to the nearest suitable aerodrome and investigate the cause, rather than automatically assuming the reason which was wrong.

Time

Time is often the crucial factor in any unwelcome scenario, either before or during flight.

Example 5: Before flight The pilot, having been held up due to road traffic congestion, arrived at the aerodrome forty minutes later than planned. Knowing that the aircraft was wanted immediately after his flight, he speeded up his pre-flight planning, and because he had planned to carry out only a short cross country flight, he did not bother to check the NOTAMS. If he had adopted the correct procedure he would have discovered that an air display was taking place at one of the aerodromes he was using as a turning point.

The next day the newspapers carried a headline: 'Fatal midair collision between a jet fighter and a light aircraft over . . . aerodrome'.

Conclusion No more need be said.

Example 6: During flight Returning from a flight which had taken much longer than planned (due to becoming lost), the pilot was in a hurry to land. During his approach to the aerodrome, and with his mind partly occupied in thinking up a less embarrassing excuse for his lateness, he forgot to carry out his aerodrome approach checks. He then carried out a very tight circuit, and while rushing through his pre-landing checks discovered that the fuel contents gauge of the selected tank was reading very low, so he quickly re-selected the opposite tank. Without realising it, he had moved the fuel selector to a half-way position, thus restricting the fuel flow.

With the selector in this position there was sufficient fuel flow available to maintain cruise power, but if full power was used, demand would exceed supply. The aircraft ahead of him carried out an extended downwind leg, and our pilot, who was pushed for time, had to follow.

However, in his haste he had not allowed enough time for the preceding aircraft to clear the runway, and he had to go around. On opening up to full throttle the engine stopped; at 200 feet the height was insufficient to enable him to reach the runway, and he had no time to discover or correct his mis-selection of the fuel system. He crashed into some trees on the approach; for him, time had run out.

Conclusion If good judgement had been used the pilot, through basic knowledge, would have appreciated that no matter how much he rushed his arrival and no matter how tight his circuit, the best he could achieve would be the saving of one or perhaps two minutes; this would have had little effect on the time he arrived in the aircraft parking area.

In this case there was plenty of fuel in the unused tank, so time in that sense had no bearing on the situation. Good judgement would also have told him that safety 'knows no compromise', and rushing through important checks while one's mind is on other things will invariably compromise safety. In any judgement situation, it is essential to get the priorities right.

The environment

The environment here means influences other than the aircraft, e.g. the weather and its associated factors, take-off and landing distances available, the terrain being overflown, etc.

Example 7: Before flight Failure to obtain or appreciate the weather situation or other pre-planning information necessary for flight, will usually mean that the flight will be undertaken with inadequate knowledge or without essential actions before flight. There are also no short cuts to planning if safety is to be reasonably assured.

During flight Let us consider the circumstances of the VFR pilot who has planned correctly in all respects bar one – the selection of suitable aerodromes which could be used as alternatives.

The flight commences without problems but unforecast weather, in the form of a lowering cloud base, later enters the scene. If the pilot sees that the lowering cloud base will prevent him maintaining his safety altitude, then he or she must decide that this is the time (yes, time enters this scenario as well) for a sensible course of action: to return or proceed to a planned alternative aerodrome, whichever is most practical, without descending below the selected safety altitude.

If this decision is not made at the correct time, the seeds of a high risk situation are inevitably sown. The VFR pilot, if he continues in the hope that the weather will improve, will only too often have to start a descent to remain in visual contact with the ground. In this case he will have to descend below his safety altitude and will start on the slippery slope to what might well be a point of no return.

In continuing to descend and remain clear of cloud, a point is only too often reached where further descent is impracticable, and on changing direction the pilot could well find that the weather has closed in behind him as well. The gamble has failed to pay off and by now, probably lost as well, he is blundering around at low level in poor visibility wishing he had never left the ground in the first place. He will have lost control of his own and his passengers' safety, and now only good luck will save the day. Only a fool gambles his life and the lives of others on lady luck.

Conclusion Sadly, this scenario can be read from many past incidents and accidents, often with fatal results. Yet the situation need never have occurred; it could have been prevented by the simple exercise of good judgement at the right time.

In all these examples the pilot, in order to exercise good judgement, would need to follow a common sequence of thoughts and actions:

- detect a circumstance;
- estimate its significance;
- choose a plan of action;
- if applicable, identify other suitable options;
- then do something, i.e. implement the decision.

Attitude development and risk management

Research on human factors in aviation operations has indicated a need to expand the traditional flight training philosophy of knowledge, skill and experience and develop new concepts as shown in Figure 11.5.

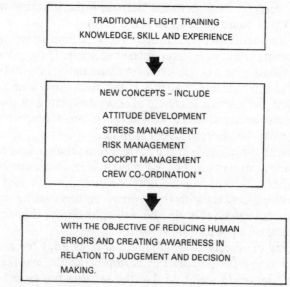

* For multi crew operations.

Fig. 11.5

Stress management has already been covered in Chapter 10. Attitude development and risk management are clearly related, as are cockpit management and crew co-ordination.

Research has identified at least six human attitudes which affect judgements and decisions. All can be found in past aircraft incidents and accidents. To protect ourselves against them we must be aware of them:

(1) anti-authority;
(2) impulsiveness;
(3) invulnerability;
(4) machismo complex;
(5) resignation;
(6) complacency.

Behavioural aspects

Anti-authority

This stems from a feeling of resentment at being told what we must or must not do. It can lead to a person disregarding regulations and required procedures. Furthermore it can become habitual, particularly if the regulations or procedures appear to be unnecessarily complex or constraining. Once this type of attitude takes over, a person is in danger of ignoring common sense and diluting, or even destroying, any ability to make a sound decision.

Everyone engaged in aviation operations will need to exert peer pressure to ensure compliance with safe operating practices, and this includes balanced objectivity and restraint when taking decisions. Safety also demands scrupulous observance of regulations and procedures, including pre-flight planning, aircraft inspection and assessment of one's own capabilities to make the flight in the existing conditions.

There is also an important message which should be considered by those who make the regulations and establish procedures. Any changes made under the emotive umbrella of safety must take into account the varying circumstances of flight situations and the workload being placed on the person who is expected to comply, whether that person is a pilot, air traffic controller, engineer etc. Regulations and procedures developed in the reasonably calm atmosphere of an office may be totally incompatible with the environment of the cockpit, air traffic control room or hangar.

Although safety is usually the stated justification for many complex rules and procedures, it would be better if we faced the fact that many are really made to enhance airspace utilisation due to commercial considerations. As a result much of today's legislation, and particularly that relating to the complex divisions of airspace, has actually made flight operations more rather than less vulnerable to human mistakes. As a result the demands on all personnel involved in aircraft operations have increased annually, and awareness of the failings of the system must also be increased to maintain the current level of safety, let alone improve it.

This situation demands reappraisal to reduce the complexity of the airspace system and make it more user friendly for all categories of flights. There is also a need for the human part of the man/machine interface to develop greater knowledge, skill and discipline, and above all a more in depth awareness of the human weaknesses which the system can only too easily magnify, to the disadvantage of safety. These two actions alone would go a long way to reducing one causal factor which encourages an anti-authority attitude.

Impulsiveness

This relates to the urge to do something immediately, when thought and time are in fact needed to arrive at a correct decision. An impulsive attitude prompts a person to do the first thing that comes to mind, without analysis of alternatives.

One difficulty in overcoming this trait is that humans learn to carry out a large number of actions or reactions which are done virtually by rote, without any cognitive reasoning. For example, a pilot knows that the throttle needs to be advanced if more power is to be obtained, an air traffic controller knows that his equipment has to be switched on before it can be used and an engineer knows that to remove a nut an appropriate spanner or similar tool will be needed. The line between impulse and instinct is very thin and a positive effort is required to differentiate between the two.

The ability to differentiate can only be developed by thoroughly appreciating that there are many occasions when a compulsive action can be hazardous, and instead, the ability to recognise the need for a thoughtful decision will be of paramount importance.

Invulnerability

This is the feeling that one cannot actually influence a situation or the outcome of a series of events. It also includes a fundamental belief in good or bad luck, and a willingness to go along with decisions and actions planned or made by others.

A number of people subconsciously think that accidents only happen to others, never themselves. While appreciating that accidents can happen, they tend to remove themselves from the good judgement connection. Pilots who adopt this attitude are more likely to take chances and incur unnecessary risks, because they do not weigh up the possibilities of a hazardous situation occurring. They will normally have a poor awareness of what might happen because of their 'it will not happen to me' syndrome.

Sensible people know that events do not always go as planned, and they remain in a continuous state of awareness as to what might happen. This preparedness, or 'situational awareness', enables them to see possible situations at an earlier stage, thus giving more time for analysis of events, possible alternatives and wiser decision making.

Machismo complex

This relates to having an excessively high opinion of oneself, and is often demonstrated by displaying conceit and arrogance. People with this behavioural attitude will usually do things on the basis of trying to prove that they are better than anyone else. They take risks to prove to themselves, as well as others, that this assumption of their abilities is correct.

In the case of pilots this often leads to them deliberately placing themselves in situations in which either their own or the aircraft's capability is exceeded, with disastrous results. Past accidents have sadly revealed that actions of this sort have cost the lives of others as well as the pilots themselves.

People who develop this exaggerated sense of ability are not welcome members of the aviation fraternity, and have extreme difficulties in controlling themselves or indeed being controlled by rules, regulations or other people.

Resignation

In this context resignation means the tendency to avoid making difficult choices or accepting responsibility. People who resign themselves to the apparent inevitable do not see themselves as making a great deal of difference in what happens to them.

When things go well, or according to plan, they tend to think 'That's good luck'. When things go badly they usually attribute it to bad luck, or feel that someone or something is out to get them. Thus they have an innate sense of leaving decisions to others, for better or worse. In essence this is a tendency to conform with group behaviour (conformity) and comply with the wishes of others (compliance). Sometimes this attitude leads to the acceptance of unreasonable or unsafe requests, in order not to appear a difficult person. They may even relinquish their pilot-in-command responsibility and accept the decisions of others rather than risk making a decision which would be unpopular with others.

This attitude shows underconfidence, and when any form of group decision is made by others there will be a natural tendency to be influenced and agree with that decision, whether or not it is a good one.

Aviators are generally gregarious by nature, so there will often be the risk of following decisions made by others. This trait of shifting one's own responsibility on to others and accepting their decisions is often called 'risky shift'. So whether or not someone has an attitude of resignation, great care must be taken when agreeing to a group decision as it is often made on a degree of compromise between individuals. In any group there may be individuals who are inclined to take higher risks than others. These could also be the more dominant in the group and might have more influence on the decisions. The moral is clear: do not be influenced by others who have less regard for the risks than you do.

Complacency

This attitude can lead to a reduced awareness of danger. The high degree of automation and reliability in current aircraft and equipment, and the routines involved in their operation, can all lead to complacency.

This trait often develops too as pilots become more experienced in a particular type of aircraft, procedure or operational activity. Its origin is found in confidence, an indispensable trait for the successful pilot. Pilots' confidence levels are determined by their past experiences, training and personalities. As a pilot's learning curve on a new aircraft begins to flatten out, decisions become easier and flying becomes more routine and automatic.

When a pilot changes to a high performance aircraft, the stresses during the transition are a strong motivator for acquiring the skills and knowledge necessary to master the new type of aircraft. As the combination of training and experience give rise to confidence, however, stress is no longer a factor and complacency frequently moves in to fill the void left by stress. Complacency, then, may be defined as a state of confidence plus contentment. The higher accident rate for pilots with 1000 to 3000 flying hours, compared to those with less flying experience, is often explained by complacency.

The earliest effects of complacency are subtle erosions of the desire to remain proficient. The pre-flight becomes less complete and more automatic. Items concerning personal safety are frequently neglected. Success in mastering his/her environment leads the pilot to become increasingly likely to play a flight by ear, rather than plan ahead for possible contingencies. Complacency seems not too far removed from 'spring fever'.

There may even be physical symptoms such as a gradual increase in weight and a general decline in physical condition caused by lack of attentiveness to health. Like a pilot who suffers from hypoxia, the complacent pilot is unaware of the gradual deterioration in personal performance and so loses the ability for critical self-appraisal. This type of behaviour can be insidious and pilots must be alert to it.

All these attitudes are aspects of human nature which anyone may exhibit at some time or other. Thoughts generated by strong feelings are a fairly natural process and can reflect on human actions. Just reading about some of the more common human attitudes should make readers aware of the inherent dangers of letting our feelings, or the opinions of others, overrule our ability to make sensible decisions.

The avoidance of these behavioural aspects will enable pilots to maintain more accurate mental models of in-flight circumstances as well as increasing their situational awareness.

Risk assessment

'If you are looking for perfect safety, you will do well to sit on a fence and watch the birds.'

Wilbur Wright 1901

But how do we know that the fence will not collapse? Only by assessing its condition before we sit on it, and even then our assessment may be wrong.

An element of risk exists in most human activities and we come to accept it as part of our daily lives, to the extent that it becomes a fundamental part of human behaviour. Nevertheless, on numerous occasions we do have the potential to recognise risk, weigh up the alternatives and come to a balanced conclusion (Fig. 11.6). The ability to do this is vital to safety in aviation, where risk cannot be completely avoided but the penalties of taking unnecessary risks can be very high.

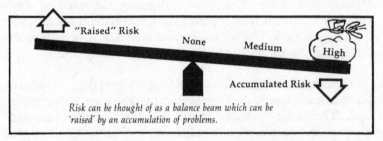

Risk can be thought of as a balance beam which can be 'raised' by an accumulation of problems.

Fig. 11.6 From AOPA Air Safety Foundation Safety Report.

To assess risk it must first be recognised, but certain risks are not recognised and the seeds of hazardous situations are sown. There is no magic formula for teaching pilots how to recognise the degree of risk they are taking, because human behaviour varies widely between individuals and situations.

Nobody is born with the ability to fly; it can be learned only through education and practice. As already mentioned there are two parts: the development of motor skills and the ability to make good decisions. In the early stages of learning it is logical to concentrate on motor skills and simple judgement, with the latter generally confined to such items as correctly positioning the aircraft in the traffic pattern, using the flying controls and throttle to achieve the correct path and speed, using the controls and judging the height of the aircraft during the landing flare, etc.

The development of more complex judgements based on multiple factors is left until later because motor skills are developed by handling items which can be seen, felt and moved, while cognitive judgements and decisions are more abstract, using intelligence and awareness.

The four basic elements involved in judgement development, already mentioned, are also involved in risk assessment: the pilot, the aircraft, the time available and environmental conditions.

The pilot

Pilot performance can be affected in many ways during a flight, and judgement can easily be clouded when stress levels are high. To refresh your memory, the four basic stressors are:

(1) *Physical stress* Conditions associated with the pilot's immediate environment, which affect physical well-being, e.g. temperature, noise, vibration, lack of oxygen, humidity.
(2) *Physiological stress* The pilot's physical condition in relation to lack of sleep, fatigue, inadequate meals etc.
(3) *Psychological stress* Emotional influences, the need to navigate, communicate with ATC, operate the aircraft and make decisions.
(4) *Sociological stress* Emotional stresses as a result of marital problems, family illness, job pressures, death of near relatives etc.

Any of these stressors can raise the risk factor during flight, so pilots must be able to assess not only their stress level but also their ability to conduct a flight. The latter includes proper pre-flight preparation and the competence and qualifications needed for the flight to be successful.

The aircraft

The risk factors of the aircraft involve its condition and suitability for the intended flight. For example, would an aircraft with a single nav/com radio and without a pitot heater be suitable for a flight in IMC? In VMC this equipment may well be sufficient, but even so a continuous process of risk assessment should take place during flight.

Then there is the important aspect of fuel. It is not just a case of filling up the tanks before flight. A pilot must calculate the fuel required to complete the flight, including sufficient to allow for a diversion, plus a reserve. Fuel calculations should be made during flight to ensure that consumption versus time is running to plan.

Although many pilots consider these aspects during pre-flight planning, they do not always realise they are part of risk assessment.

The environment

This is a wide-reaching risk element and covers situations which might limit or modify the pilot's decisions: the prevailing and anticipated weather, and the regulations governing the operation of the aircraft within the airspace system.

Time

Time has a controlling influence on the other three elements. In flight the passage of time can easily be overlooked by a pilot who is totally involved in resolving a flight problem. When time is short, or perceived to be short, impulsive or inappropriate decisions are more easily made. Lack of time does not just add to risk, it multiplies it, and the shorter the time available the more likely that risks will be increased.

These four factors, which are involved in every flight, can join and accumulate in a variety of ways. It is the pilot's function to analyse continually the progress of every flight, and to reduce or remove the adverse effects of increasing risk by taking positive and correct decisions. In many cases simple actions, such as turning back or diverting at an early stage when weather deterioration is increasing the risk, will suffice. While such action may create inconvenience or social problems, these should not be allowed to influence the safety of the flight. A bad decision to press on because of time, travel or social commitments may well result in a permanent release from all of them for ever.

Accidents

Summaries of past incidents and accidents show quite clearly that a lack of motor skills or perceptual judgement is a much smaller causal factor than a lack of cognitive judgement.

Among approach and landing accidents there were many occasions when the aircraft was perfectly serviceable, the weather was fine, the pilot was in current flying practice on the aircraft type, and the landing was being made on an aerodrome which had been used by the pilot on frequent occasions; yet the aircraft finished up by running out of runway and crashing through the far hedge. These accidents occurred to qualified pilots whose total flying hours ranged from hundreds to thousands. The pilots had all demonstrated their ability to land safely on hundreds of occasions and there were no mitigating circumstances. Therefore one can only conclude that they were victims of the compulsion brought about by pressures of pride, time, complacency or by carelessness, as all these accidents could have been avoided if the pilots had used good cognitive judgement and decided to go round again.

Among take-off accidents the records show that many aircraft failed to become airborne in the take-off run available and finished up in the far hedge, or stalled just outside the aerodrome boundary. It would therefore

again appear that compulsion, carelessness or complacency must figure
very high when accidents of this sort take place. In addition there may also
be a lack of knowledge relating to the take-off and landing performance of
the aircraft, which the pilot had either not been taught or had failed to
understand.

This shows the need to understand how human factors affect our
thinking processes and physical actions when we fly. We do not need a
degree in psychology or to be a qualified physician to make the effort to
understand ourselves and our attitudes and reactions to flight situations.
This will make us more aware of how to avoid many of the pitfalls and
errors to which humans are prone.

In order to do this we must continuously remember that judgement and
decisions are concerned with people, their attitudes, aspirations and social
and employment influences. In aviation they also involve the effects of
operating in an environment very different from the one in which a
human being normally lives. When a pilot steps into the cockpit he has to
adapt and reassess his thought processes, knowing that even small
mistakes can lead to hazardous consequences.

Pilots who fly with awareness that they are humans first and pilots
second, will be less at risk from human error and will automatically
improve the safety of their flight operations and be more capable of
demonstrating their 'pilot-in-command' responsibilities.

Risk management

Managing risk involves good judgement and decision making, which is all
about the way we think – or do not think. Consider these important
questions:

(1) Do you think enough?
(2) Do you think correctly?

As an example of (1), we know that many pilots are careful to fit a cover
to the pitot head when leaving the aircraft, to prevent the ingress of
insects, blowing dust etc. But what about the fuel vent? Many pilots do
not seem to give much thought of a blockage to this. Yet, while the aircraft
will fly perfectly well with an unserviceable air speed indicator, it will not
fly for long when the engine quits due to fuel starvation. Has this occurred
to you?

In the case of (2), many pilots are more worried than any manufacturer
about the use of the carburettor hot air system, and possible detonation
when the engine is at high power. Yet the same pilots are quite happy to
take-off following a magneto check which reveals a lack of an RPM drop

during the engine run-up procedure at nominal power. The two most common causes for no drop in the RPM during this procedure are that one side of the ignition system is not grounded properly, or the magneto timing is too far advanced. If the latter, the result can be destructive detonation and the aircraft should not be flown until the fault is rectified. Were you aware of this?

Another example of whether pilots are thinking correctly or enough concerns the fuel flow check carried out on aircraft with two fuel tanks which have to be selected individually.

In this case the standard procedure is to start up and taxy on one tank, then select the other and carry out the power checks before take-off. Provided the engine runs properly on each tank, most pilots assume they have checked the fuel system and it is satisfactory. But in fact all they have proved is that the rate of fuel flow from each tank is sufficient to allow the engine to operate on one tank at 1200–1500 RPM when taxying, and on the other at 1700–2000 RPM during the power checks. This has not proved that the rate of flow from either tank to the engine is adequate to meet the engine's demand at cruise power and, even more important, the engine's demand at full power during take-off. Thus the flight commences on an 'inference formed' belief that the fuel flow will be satisfactory for all normal stages of flight.

While the aircraft manufacturer ensures that the fuel lines are large enough to meet the full power demand, and fits a filter at the tank opening to the fuel line, there is no assurance that the filter will remain unblocked, or that kinks or damage to the fuel lines will not occur at some time during the life of the aircraft. So we could have a situation where the rate of fuel flow is satisfactory at lower power settings but will not meet demand at the highest power setting. Fortunately if this situation occurs in a small aircraft the shortness of the fuel lines will usually cause the engine to stop before or just after full power is applied, and before the aircraft has become airborne.

Assuming there is no problem with the rate of fuel flow from the tank selected for take-off, the other tank has yet to be proved. It is common practice to change tanks during a flight, following which the pilot may have no need to use full power unless a go-around during the approach to landing is required. It is then that the potential hazard exists. If the second fuel tank system is unable to meet the demand at full power, the pilot will be faced with engine failure at very low height and with no time to rectify it. Have you ever considered this risk?

Avoiding it is not difficult; simply ensure that full power is used during flight for at least thirty seconds after re-selecting a fuel tank, and before conducting the aerodrome approach checks.

If the flight only involves circuits, a wise pilot will avoid situations where he has to change during pre-landing checks to a tank unproven at full power; apart from the possibility of fuel cock mis-selection, he might find himself in a hazardous situation during an enforced go-around or immediately following a 'touch and go' landing, when full power is applied.

These examples show some of the typical thinking actions required if good judgements are to be developed in standard, straightforward procedures.

Take-off, approach and landing

Over 60% of aviation accidents and incidents are associated with take-off, approach and landing. Out of the 196 reported accidents to fixed wing aircraft in the UK during 1988, 37 occurred during take-off and 112 during approach and landing. The total UK accidents to rotary wing aircraft during 1988 was 27, of which 6 occurred during take-off and 10 during approach and landing.

Many occurred because the pilots lacked knowledge of the important factors affecting take-off or landing performances, e.g. the effects of wind, temperature, mass, surface conditions, lift-off speed, etc. Where these effects were known, they were not properly appreciated or calculated. Other causal factors involved hazardous thought patterns such as compulsiveness, invulnerability and complacency, indicating that these human traits are probably the most important to avoid when it comes to reducing risks. Do you think enough? Do you think correctly?

The following short summaries of actual accidents during take-off and landing highlight a need for a better understanding of both aircraft and pilot performance. Too often pilots act against good judgement and make unwise decisions, or make the right decisions too late. Most landing accidents of the sort shown would not have occurred if the pilot had used good judgement and initiated a go-around at the right time. These examples also show compulsion as a trait which often overrides good judgement, just when it is most needed.

Take-off 'A/C hit hedge during T/O. A/C destroyed – minor injuries only. The pilot was attempting a curved approach to a short, wet, sloping grass field. The approach was badly judged and the A/C touched down long and fast and decision to stop or "go-around" was delayed.'

'A/C hit a fence on T/O from a short stubble field. No injury.'

'A/C overran following aborted T/O. Possible brake failure. Pilot abandoned T/O due poor acceleration. Both the toe brakes and parking brakes were ineffective. The A/C overran into a wooden fence and subsequently halted with the LH wing on fire. Subsequent examination of the brake units failed to reveal any pre-existing defects.'

'A/C crashed on T/O – wing torn off. No serious injuries. The airfield state generally was very soft with boggy patches.'

'A/C failed to get airborne, overran and nosed over. Nil injuries. Despite using the full R/W and short field T/O technique the A/C failed to gain sufficient speed. The T/O was aborted but due to the wet and soft surface conditions the A/C could not be stopped before the R/W end. The A/C ran into a ploughed field and overturned. A calculation subsequent to the accident indicates that a take-off run in excess of 500 metres would have been required in the prevailing conditions, soft R/W with long grass. The actual T/O run available was 458 metres although the R/W length was 553 metres.'

Landing 'A/C overran short wet grass R/W. NLG collapsed. No injury. The pilot diverted due to poor WX at his destination A/D. The A/C was landed on a wet grass R/W with an available landing distance of 370 metres. Despite making his approach using a short field technique he landed slightly long and overran through a fence. The pilot reports that the braking action was "almost non-existent".'

Why Didn't He Go Round? The answer to this question is the key to many an overrun accident. There's no disgrace in going round again even the best pilots do it!

'A/C overran into field and overturned. Minor injuries to two onboard. Following a high approach the aircraft landed well down the runway.

The pilot then decided to go-around and applied full power. The aircraft swung off the runway into an adjoining ploughed field and overturned.'

'A/C overran on landing. No injury. A/C overran and nosewheel entered ditch causing substantial damage. The pilot applied the brakes but with reportedly little effect. The grass R/W was subsequently found to be very wet. R/W marks also indicate that touchdown point was some 140 metres into the 440 metre strip.'

'Pilot misjudged approach and overran into river. Nil injuries. Approach was made through smoke blowing across the runway. Landing direction chosen to avoid tailwind component on the reciprocal. Touchdown was at approx halfway down the R/W. Braking action was poor on wet grass.'

'A/C overshot R/W on landing, hit hedge and overturned. Minor injuries. Following an approach to runway 08 surface wind135/10KTS the aircraft landed half-way down the runway. Having bounced on touchdown the pilot attempted a go-around but the aircraft hit a boundary hedge and came down on the road beyond.'

Weather related risks

Weather has always been, and no doubt will continue to be, a problem in aviation operations, although weather related accidents (excluding difficult wind conditions on take-off and landing) are relatively low in numerical terms, (UK 13 in 1988), they are high in relation to serious injuries or fatalities.

From the psychological standpoint the greatest risk stems from people interpreting the likelihood of the meteorological forecast being right or wrong in accordance with their preference at the time. (Preference in this case being current external pressures.) Thus on a number of occasions the 'Go' or 'No Go' decision is determined by factors other than the forecast weather. It is vital to your risk management to base your decisions purely on the weather and your own ability, rather than allow current needs and commitments to dictate your decision to take-off.

Another important factor in the avoidance of weather related accidents, which is regrettably often ignored, is 'safety altitude'. This, as the name implies, is the lowest altitude at which you should fly during poor visibility or a low cloud base. To guard against worsening weather during a navigation flight, a safety altitude should always be established during pre-flight planning. A commonly used formula is to plan for an altitude at least 1000 feet higher than any ground or obstructions within 5 nm of the intended track, although this may have to be amended when operating under the floor of regulated airspace.

Establishing a safe altitude shows sensible judgement of risk, should the weather deteriorate en route. However, different pilots use safety altitude in different ways. For example, a pilot qualified in instrument flying may choose to fly the route below the safety altitude with the intention of climbing up to, or above, the chosen safety altitude should the weather deteriorate.

This would be a risky procedure for the non-instrument qualified pilot, who can only put safety altitude to good effect by not flying below it until his destination is in sight; otherwise, if the cloud base lowers to below the safety altitude, the pilot will be trapped underneath, probably in worsening weather conditions. To a non-instrument qualified pilot, a safety altitude will only be effective in managing risks if he or she can make a decision to turn back or divert before getting into a high risk situation. Many pilots during navigation flights have failed to appreciate that deteriorating weather can close in from either side of the aircraft's route, and not only from ahead.

Finally regarding weather, pilots who fly at or above safety altitude can more quickly decide when to turn back or divert if lowering cloud is the problem. In effect they will have made the decision on the ground before the flight: if they cannot maintain their safety altitude, they must not 'press on'.

You will find it useful to think up some scenarios of your own; your ability to assess and manage risk will automatically improve, particularly if the scenarios are discussed with fellow pilots. Bear in mind that in balancing risk the two main components are:

(1) *Intellectual* – using the knowledge you possess, and this may not always be correct or sufficient to enable your information processing system to work efficiently.
(2) *Motivational* – your attitude towards risk and how it is affected by other influences and pressures, e.g. the need to get home, peer pressure etc.

A pilot who has developed superior skill and good judgement will use his good judgement to minimise the need for the use of his superior skill.

Cockpit management and crew co-ordination

Poor management of cockpit activities commonly leads to frustration and distractions, which in turn can lead to serious incidents or accidents. This is particularly so with weather related problems during navigation flights or when an equipment malfunction occurs.

Organising the cockpit workload starts on the ground, and while the facilities for pre-flight preparation vary widely depending on where the flight commences, it is essential to obtain any information pertinent to the flight on:

- actual and anticipated weather;
- aerodrome/destination and alternate facilities;
- en-route aspects;
- aircraft operating data.

Pilots are taught how to glean this information from different sources and put it to practical use. Pilots should also consider the number of tasks to be performed during the flight, ensuring as far as possible that these are spread properly so that several tasks do not have to be done at the same time. This sounds easier than it is, but it is not too difficult to rationalise cockpit actions so that they become more of a continuous flow than sudden bursts of activity.

For example, during a navigation trip it is unnecessary continuously to identify ground features or check position by radio navigation aids. Depending on the type of route, position checks every 5, 10 or even 15 minutes are normally adequate. This gives a more relaxed atmosphere in the cockpit, with reasonable time between position checks to attend to other routine matters such as noting fuel contents, consumption rates, engine and equipment readings etc. Furthermore, it allows time for mental activity in a calmer atmosphere, more conducive to qualified judgements or decisions should the unexpected occur.

Organising this one facet of the cockpit workload in a sensible fashion will allow a pilot to more easily maintain a state of 'situational awareness' during flight.

Multi-crew operations

Evidence suggests that 70% of incidents and accidents in the public transport sector are caused, at least in part, by the flightcrew failing to work together effectively. Studies show that problems during multi-crew operations often have little to do with the technical aspects of operating the aircraft or its equipment, but are mainly associated with poor decision making, problem solving and judgement.

Many mistakes have resulted from ineffective communication; poor situational awareness; and inadequate emphasis on team management. For years aircrew training has concentrated on the technical aspects of flying with pilots trained to operate the aircraft with precision but not trained in inter-personal communications and cockpit management skills.

Nowadays, when flying duties are shared by more than one pilot, crew co-ordination is vital. One might think that employing two pilots in the cockpit will reduce the pilot workload, and while this is true, it does introduce other factors which may lead to mistakes.

Integrated functions and delegated duties have to be carried out by each member of the flightcrew. This involves co-ordinated team work in the exchange of information and cross checking, to ensure that cockpit duties and procedures are performed correctly. It normally requires a 'procedure guide' which is a listing of all the actions individual crew members have to perform. This procedure uses a 'challenge and response' system which requires one flightcrew member to call out the required action and another to implement it while being checked (when feasible) by the caller.

The pilot designated as captain has overall responsibility for flightcrew actions but the standard of information exchange depends heavily on the attitude and co-operation of the flightcrew. Some blocks to communication are pre-occupation, resentment, status differential or strongly held opinions.

The following incident is an example of how things can go wrong when two pilots are working together as a team. It is an actual event where a failure in the cross checking of one pilot's actions by another could have led to disaster.

The flight was in VMC on an IFR flight plan. Prior to take-off the altimeters were set by the pilot-in-command in accordance with the ATIS information. At the same time, the co-pilot who had been assigned the navigation tasks was busy selecting the approach chart for the aircraft's destination airport.

After take-off and approaching the assigned altitude, the air traffic controller called to say that the aircraft had climbed through the assigned altitude according to his Mode C transponder information. Because the altimeters showed that the aircraft was still below the assigned altitude, the crew immediately suspected the accuracy of the Mode C information, particularly as the aircraft transponder had been snagged on a previous flight. At this stage the transponder was switched off.

However, the transponder was actually serviceable and the error had occurred because the pilot-in-command had set 1012 mb on the altimeters instead of 1021 mb. Although in this case the real cause was discovered shortly afterwards, the flightcrew had already made three errors:

(1) The pilot-in-command had set the wrong QNH on both altimeters.
(2) The co-pilot had failed to cross check the actions of the pilot-in-command.
(3) Both pilots had fallen into the trap of assuming the transponder was inaccurate, because of its previously recorded unserviceability. This assumption is often referred to as a type of 'confirmation bias' i.e. a preference or inclination which tends to inhibit impartial judgement leading to real events being ignored and replaced by incorrect assumptions.

Instead of assuming that the transponder was inaccurate, the pilots should have double checked the altimeter sub-scale setting before deciding why the altimeter reading and the controller's Mode C readout were at odds.

Training
Training programmes such as Line-Orientated Flight Training (LOFT) and Cockpit Resource Management (CRM) are specially designed and used by the operators of larger aircraft, and this basic manual will not dwell on this subject except to say that CRM skills are developed through LOFT training procedures normally conducted in advanced flight simulators. Complete flightcrews, using representative flights on a real time basis, practise normal, abnormal and emergency operations as a team. The purpose of this training is not to test competence, but to allow flightcrews to develop and learn how to work effectively together in all situations.

The following is an extract from the multi-crew training requirements established by the Flightcrew Licensing Working Group (FCL) of the European Civil Aviation Conference (ECAC) in its work towards the harmonisation of pilot licences within Europe:

'Practical instruction for crew co-ordination and co-operation in the operation of multi-crew certificated aeroplanes. This instruction shall cover the following:

(a) objectives of crew co-ordination concept, division of tasks between pilot flying (PF) and pilot not flying (PNF), use of checklists under normal, abnormal and emergency operational conditions, mutual supervision, information and support, call out procedures;

(b) pre-flight preparation including documentation, computation of take-off performance data;

(c) pre-flight checks including radio and navigation equipment checks and setting;

(d) before take-off checks including powerplant check, and crew take-off briefing by PF;

(e) normal take-offs with different flap settings, tasks of PF and PNF, call-outs;

(f) rejected take-offs, cross wind take-offs, take-offs with maximum take-off mass, engine failure after V1;

(g) normal and abnormal operation of aircraft systems, use of checklist;

(h) emergency procedures including engine failure and fire, smoke control and removal, windshear during take-off and landing, emergency descent, incapacitation of a flight crew member;

(i) early recognition of and reaction on approaching stall speeds under differing aircraft configurations;

(j) instrument flight procedures including holding procedures, ILS approaches using raw navigation data, flight director and automatic pilot, one-engine-out approaches, NDB/VOR approaches and circling approaches; approach briefing by PF, setting of navigation equipment, call-out procedures during approaches;

(k) go arounds, normal and with one-engine out, rejected landing support of the PF by the PNF;

(l) landings, normal, crosswind and with one-engine-out; transition from instrument flight to visual flight after reaching decision height or minimum descent height;

(m) skill test with emphasis on the application of the crew coordination concept.'

This outline shows the current thinking of the European Civil Aviation Administrations and International Aviation Organisations on the type of training considered appropriate for multi-crew co-ordination. But even with specific training there are no simple answers to the problems of crew co-ordination, although a professional approach goes a long way to avoiding them.

This means a business-like approach to the pilot's role, putting personal pre-judgement of others to one side and ignoring status differentials when doubt exists as to whether a particular action has been properly done or a mis-judgement has been made.

Whether operating as a single pilot or multi-crew, it is essential to apportion cockpit tasks in relation to time. Many pilots have come to grief because of a self-imposed increase in workload at an inappropriate moment, when attention has had to be concentrated on actually flying the aircraft. It is at moments like these that additional cockpit tasks may be carried out in the wrong order, or missed altogether, and the chances of a mis-selection of system controls are increased.

Provided pilots are one second ahead of the aircraft they will be in control of the situation, but if pilots allow themselves to get one second behind the aircraft a breeding ground for mistakes will be created. It is only by planning ahead and doing what is required at the right time, that a state of 'situational awareness' can be maintained and the chances of making mistakes reduced.

Cockpit ergonomics

A pilot's cockpit should be 'user friendly', but sadly this is not easy to achieve. Apart from the difficulties of designing a cockpit layout compatible with different sizes of pilot, there will also be the important constraint of financial costs. While designers pay attention to the hazards of badly sited system controls and switches, there are many aircraft in which it would appear that commercial considerations have been given priority over human factors.

Man is very adaptable and able to compensate for many design inadequacies, but the closer the aircraft's qualities match man's capabilities, the less chance there is of mistakes being made by the pilot and the higher the level of safety.

Workspace constraints

Although pilots should not hesitate to inform their airworthiness authorities when they discover a design fault in the location of system controls, switches, etc., there is little they can do in the short term except to familiarise themselves with them and adopt their own measures to overcome design deficiencies. Continuous awareness will be needed during flight to avoid the selection of the wrong lever or switch, or the misinterpretation of instrument readings.

With regard to the pilot's seating position and posture, it is obviously advisable to ensure that the seat is adjusted for the pilot's comfort and securely locked in position. After adjusting the harness to fit firmly around the body, pilots should check their ability to reach and operate all necessary controls, switches, etc. and should make sure that the instruments can be clearly read.

Cockpit visibility

For structural reasons it is impossible for a designer to provide uninterrupted visibility all round an aircraft. This can reduce the pilot's ability to lookout but the effect can be minimised by moving the upper torso and head; this should be developed into a natural and frequent habit. Many pilots think low wing aircraft allow a better lookout than high wing aircraft, but in practice the pilot will not be able to see through the wing, wherever it is. The direction of the threat from the opposing aircraft is the most important factor in all 'near miss' or 'midair' situations, so pilots cannot afford to feel more safe and relax their vigilance just because they are flying a low wing type.

In relation to workspace design and cockpit fenestration, the UK syllabus for Human Performance and Limitations includes the term 'anthropometry', defined as:

'the study of, or technique for measuring the various sizes and proportions of the human body, for use in anthropological classification and comparison.'

Anthropometry is obviously relevant to the design of the cockpit or flight deck, and therefore within the domain of the aircraft designer and manufacturer rather than the individual pilot. Perhaps the word 'ergonomics' might have been more relevant as it refers to workers and their environment in relation to biology and engineering. Either term could be used to draw the pilot's attention to the difficulties of designing the pilot's workplace in a manner which reduces the likelihood of human error.

Misinterpretation of instruments

The same principles must apply when designing aircraft instruments and positioning them in the cockpit. Here again professional and particularly private pilots (the latter being over 60% of pilots) do not normally have much access to the manufacturers. They have to learn to be aware of and to compensate for any problems resulting from the design or positioning of the instruments.

Great strides have been made in the displays modern instruments give, but inevitably problems remain. The three needle display altimeter is probably the easiest instrument for misinterpretation, and pilots would be wise to build into their procedures the 'check and double check' principle when reading the altimeter, and setting or re-setting its sub-scale.

Apart from the poor presentation of the three needle display altimeter, another possible cause of misinterpretation lies in the fact that pilots are trained not to stare at individual cockpit instruments. There are several reasons for this, such as the need to maintain a good lookout. Therefore we should bear in mind that a pilot will on most occasions already know the altitude being flown, and will probably only glance at the altimeter for a few seconds at a time to monitor and correct any altitude deviation. So quick glances at the altimeter become a habit. However, the initial determination of altimeter reading will need more time. As an example, try reading the altimeters in Fig 11.7, giving yourself just 5 seconds for each. This exercise will show the difficulties of interpreting the correct indications from this type of altimeter. The correct answers are given at the foot of page 150.

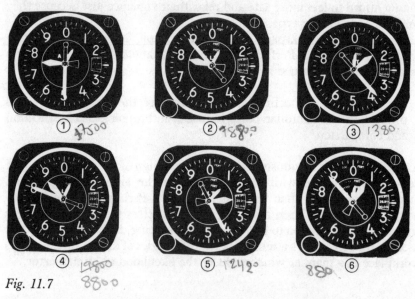

Fig. 11.7

There are still aircraft, particularly in the general aviation sector, equipped with the old style artificial horizon. This gives a roll and bank display which can easily be misinterpreted by anyone used to the more modern attitude indicator. A pilot could quite easily mis-read it and think

Fig. 11.8 Some earlier type artificial horizon instruments have a bank pointer at the top of the instrument case which indicates degrees of bank in the opposite sense to the actual direction of bank and this can be confusing

he or she was banked to the right, when they were actually rolling or banking to the left. A similar situation could apply to a pilot used to the old style artificial horizon instrument, when flying an aircraft fitted with the modern attitude indicator. This is shown in Figures 11.8 and 11.9.

Fig. 11.9 In the case of the more modern attitude indicator the bank pointer is synchronised with the direction of turn

VOR instrument displays have changed radically over the years, and the presentation of information varies with different manufacturers and the year of production. Some of these changes are fairly obvious and should present no problems to the pilot. But there are some displays in which the omni bearing selector (OBS) indications are read from the bottom of the dial, and others in which they are read from the top. This again can lead to confusion, particularly when both types are combined on the same instrument panel.

It is therefore important to check and double check when setting the OBS or reading the degrees of bearing which have been selected. It is also advisable to use the double check procedure when carrying out other actions in the cockpit, particularly the positioning of the flap and landing gear controls. Although manufacturers now give them different shapes, pilots still manage to select the wrong one with embarrassing results.

The same applies to the positioning and shape of the mixture control and carburettor heat control. Again, despite these normally being a different shape, pilots still manage to reach out and operate the wrong one, often with disastrous results. When planning to descend, carburettor heat should always be selected before reducing power. This is a fail-safe procedure because inadvertent selection of the mixture control would immediately result in a complete loss of power. This would not be so clearly recognised if a significantly reduced power had been selected before the mixture control.

There are other instruments besides altimeters, attitude indicators and navaids which can cause confusion. One example is the combined RPM indicators often used in multi-engine aircraft. In these one instrument combines the RPM needles of the left and right engines, and this can be difficult to interpret when reading the indications quickly.

Colour coded instruments   In recent years the introduction of colour to instrument displays has been extremely helpful to pilots, notably in such instruments as the airspeed indicator, engine oil and temperature gauges and cylinder head temperature gauges.

One advantage of colour on the airspeed indicator is the reduced need to remember a number of numerical figures such as flap limiting speed, maximum rough air speed, single engine best climbing speed etc. Another advantage is that colour also acts as an 'attention getter', enabling a pilot to more easily see and react in certain situations.

However, many of the earlier aircraft still flying today are not equipped with colour coded instruments and pilots must study the aircraft flight manual or equivalent to learn the appropriate figures needed to operate the aircraft safely. In Europe it is fairly common to find some aircraft instruments calibrated in kilometres per hour as well as knots and statute miles, and great care must be exercised to avoid misinterpretation.

All pilots must confirm the type of presentation used in any instrument and must pay particular attention to avoid misinterpretation during flight. It is also important during pre-flight checks to ensure that all instruments and placards are fully visible.

Aircraft manuals and placards
Most aircraft flight manuals or operating handbooks require certain placards to be clearly exhibited in the cockpit. These contain warning information which the manufacturer or airworthiness authorities consider should be highlighted so that the pilot can operate the aircraft safely. Some contain information relating to emergencies and it is important that pilots know exactly where this can be found, to avoid any delay in an emergency.

Every effort should be made to avoid misinterpretation of warning information. Cockpit placards cannot contain lengthy information so pilots must spend sufficient time studying the aircraft manual to ensure they fully understand the rather terse statements which placards normally contain.

It is a sad fact of life that most of us are guilty of misinterpreting what we read from time to time and this can occur when reading aircraft manuals. For example, a number of pilots have been known to glance at range and endurance figures given in the performance section of the aircraft manual, but have failed to appreciate that the figures are based on

---

ANSWERS TO ALTIMETER QUIZ

(1) 7,500 ft. (2) 7,880 ft. (3) 1,380 ft. (4) 8,800 ft. (5) 12,420 ft. (6) 880 ft.

proper mixture leaning techniques, and so have run out of fuel before reaching their destination.

Let us consider the case of the pilot who has carefully worked out his fuel consumption figures for a given trip, but upsets his calculations while in flight. For example, having selected a good economical cruising airspeed he runs late on departure and to make up time he decides to

Pressure altitude ft	RPM	20°C below standard temp			Standard temperature			20°C above standard temp		
		% BHP	KTAS	GPH	% BHP	KTAS	GPH	% BHP	KTAS	GPH
2000	2400	–	–	–	75	100	6.1	70	99	5.7
	2300	71	96	5.7	66	95	5.4	63	94	5.1
	2200	62	91	5.1	59	90	4.8	56	89	4.6
	2100	55	86	4.5	● 53	85	4.3 ●	51	84	4.2
	2000	49	80	4.1	47	79	3.9	46	78	3.8
4000	2450	–	–	–	75	102	6.1	70	101	5.7
	2400	76	101	6.1	71	100	5.7	67	99	5.4
	2300	67	95	5.4	63	94	5.1	60	93	4.9
	2200	60	90	4.8	56	89	4.6	54	88	4.4
	2100	53	85	4.4	51	84	4.2	49	83	4.0
	2000	48	80	3.9	46	78	3.8	45	77	3.7
6000	2500	–	–	–	75	104	6.1	71	103	5.7
	2400	72	100	5.8	67	99	5.4	64	98	5.2
	2300	64	95	5.2	60	94	4.9	57	93	4.7
	2200	57	89	4.6	54	88	4.4	52	87	4.3
	2100	51	84	4.2	49	83	4.0	48	82	3.9
	2000	46	79	3.8	45	78	3.7	44	76	3.6
8000	2550	–	–	–	75	106	6.1	71	105	5.7
	2500	76	104	6.2	71	103	5.8	67	102	5.4
	2400	68	99	5.5	64	98	5.2	61	97	4.9
	2300	61	94	5.0	58	93	4.7	55	92	4.5
	2200	55	89	4.5	52	87	4.3	51	86	4.2
	2100	49	83	4.1	48	82	3.9	46	81	3.8
10,000	2500	72	103	5.8	68	102	5.5	64	101	5.2
	2400	65	98	5.3	61	97	5.0	58	96	4.8
	2300	58	93	4.7	56	92	4.5	53	91	4.4
	2200	53	88	4.3	51	86	4.2	49	85	4.0
	2100	48	82	4.0	46	81	3.9	45	79	3.8
12,000	2450	65	100	5.3	62	99	5.0	59	98	4.8
	2400	62	97	5.0	59	96	4.8	56	95	4.6
	2300	56	92	4.6	54	91	4.4	52	90	4.3
	2200	51	87	4.2	49	85	4.1	48	84	4.0
	2100	47	81	3.9	45	80	3.8	44	78	3.7

Conditions 1670 Pounds. Recommended lean mixture (See Section 4, Cruise).
Note Cruise speeds are shown for an airplane equipped with speed fairings which increase the speeds by approximately two knots.

Fig. 11.10

increase the cruising power. To see the results of this, look at some actual consumption figures applicable to a typical light aeroplane.

Figure 11.10 shows that the aircraft, when flown in ISA conditions and with lean mixture, uses 4.3 gallons per hour at 2000 feet and 53% power. If the flight was planned for this power setting and altitude, the aircraft, with full tanks, would have an endurance of 5.6 hours and a range of 476 nm in still air, based on a usable fuel quantity of 24.5 gallons. However, if the pilot now decides to open up to 75% power the endurance would reduce to 4 hours and the range in still air will become 400 nm. In addition, at 75% power it is unlikely that mixture leaning technique would be used and the approximate endurance figure would actually be reduced to just over 3 hours and the range would be nearer to 300 nm with significant reduction in flight safety.

A second example of misinterpretation concerns a commonly held erroneous belief that the mixture control must not be used below an altitude of 5000 feet in normally aspirated engines with float type carburettors. This false understanding stems from the engine manufacturers' recommendations that mixture leaning techniques should not be implemented below an altitude of 5000 feet when using power in excess of approximately 70%. The key words in this recommendation are 'when using power in excess of 70%'. The figure of 5000 feet comes from the fact that in a normally aspirated aero engine, power over 70% cannot be obtained above 5000 feet due to decreasing air density.

Therefore true facts are that mixture leaning techniques can be implemented to any altitude provided that not more than 70% power is being used.

Note 1   The figure of 5000 feet altitude has now been lowered to 3000 feet because of the use of 100 LL fuel which has given rise to some plug fouling problems.

Note 2   The figure of 70% power varies slightly with the particular engine being used.

These examples show how misinterpretations come about, and also the need to read the manufacturers' recommendations very carefully.

Other methods, besides placards act as 'attention getting' stimuli to give warning information to the pilot, for example stall warners in the form of a light or aural system. However, pilots should not rely on these because, in the case of stall warning lights, they are often adjacent to the airspeed indicator and a pilot sufficiently distracted not to monitor the reading of the airspeed indicator is hardly likely to be looking in the direction of the stall warning light. Aural stall warnings often tend to be subdued, particularly when operated pneumatically, and if a pilot is wearing a headset in a busy ATC environment, the warning can easily be missed.

Use of checklists

Great care is taken in the preparation of checklists for the commercial air transport sector, but the checklists for general aviation activities are sadly not written with the frailties of human nature in mind.

Nevertheless, checklists do play an important part in safety, and supplement human memory. In earlier days small aircraft were very simple in design, with sparse instrument panels and little in the way of operating systems or equipment; it was not difficult for pilots to use short mnemonics as a memory aid to carry out the necessary checks and procedures.

Today large numbers of small aircraft of more complex design are fitted with a relatively large number of instruments, systems and avionic equipment. Added to this are the many privileges given to the largest number of pilots, who fall within the general aviation sector, so that today we have an aviation environment which necessitates the use of checklists from the very beginning of a pilot's training.

But there are many checklists which abound with traps for the unwary, or for those who have not spent sufficient time studying the aircraft manual for the specific type being flown. These traps range from having two or three check items on one line, to giving insufficient information for all checks and drills to be properly carried out for the safe operation of the aircraft. While checklists should be short and to the point, they must carry sufficient information to ensure that important actions are not omitted.

In addition, flying instructors in particular should note that the manufacturer designs aircraft checklists for qualified pilots. When used by student pilots, their value as attention getters and memory joggers will inevitably be reduced. This can be overcome in training by supplementing the manufacturer's checklist to ensure that the student is not only reminded about the item to be checked, but also understands what action is required. For example, some checklists simply list items in columns, and in the action column have the word 'check' against each item – hardly a satisfactory way of indicating what action should be taken.

When more than one item is included on the same line, the danger is that the pilot will read off the first item, carrying out the action required, and will then automatically drop down to the next line, missing one or two items. This mistake is far more common than many pilots realise.

Finally, there is always the danger of using checklists like a shopping list. There will always be points of operating procedures which are not identified on checklists in small aircraft. For example, under the heading of power checks the words 'in a clear area' or 'clear of rough ground' will appear, but never the words 'ensure there is no debris or very small stones in the vicinity of the propeller'. This is an important consideration because particles can be sucked up and can produce insidious damage to the propeller blades, eventually causing hair line cracks. This type of blade damage is not easily recognised during pre-flight inspections, but can lead to a separation of part of the blade when under stress – hardly pleasant if it happens just after take-off.

A further example is the checklist for checks prior to take-off. A list of individual items will be shown, but sooner or later the pilot will come to the line which mentions 'instruments' or 'flight instruments'. This encompasses a number of items to be checked, without itemising each one in turn. A pilot who has previously been fed each item is now left to rely on memory alone, making it more likely that something will be forgotten or performed incorrectly.

When a checklist is needed, each item to be checked or each action taken should be clearly listed separately. If this is not done the pilot should be fully aware that certain checks must be recalled from memory. A pilot who appreciates the weak points of checklists will have a strengthened situational awareness and will be more likely to use good judgement when performing checks and drills.

Bear in mind that situational awareness is a constant and accurate perception of the factors and conditions that affect the aircraft and flightcrew. In other words it is knowing what is going on around you, and the higher your state of situational awareness the lower the risk.

In conclusion

Hopefully the information in this manual will not only supplement your existing knowledge, but will also strengthen your awareness of human weaknesses and how they can affect your endeavours to become a safe pilot.

Sadly it is easy for training to be seen as an end in itself. However, although flight training provides a pilot applicant with the required knowledge and skills to qualify for a licence, certificate or rating, just completing the required training and test is not the end, but just the beginning.

When a pilot steps into an aircraft, he or she will need to combine the technical knowledge, skills and procedures acquired both during and after training. Another most important requirement is to know yourself and how you can make mistakes, particularly under stress. Equipped with this knowledge, the ability to think through flight situations in a sensible way will be the hallmark of any competent pilot.

A better understanding of how our physical condition and psychological processes interact with the various aspects of operating an aircraft, will improve our performance and the safety of our passengers and ourselves, as well as providing fulfilment and pleasure from flying activities. This applies whether we fly for recreation or to earn a living.

Pilots need aircraft in order to fly, but to fly safely pilots must have the ability not only to control their aircraft and its equipment, but also to control themselves and their thought processes. Without this the pilot becomes the most fail/fail system in the aircraft.

Bibliography

Official Publications

International Civil Aviation Organisation (ICAO)

Human Factors Digests
  (1) Fundamental Human Factors Concepts
  (2) Flightcrew Training
  (3) Training of Operational Personnel in Human Factors
Bulletin – Aviation Safety, October 1988
Circular – Pilot skills to make 'lookout' more effective in visual collision
          avoidance
Accident Reporting System
Accident Prevention Manual

Federal Aviation Administration (FAA) (US)

Drug hazards in aviation medicine
Aviation news publications

FAA and Transport Canada

Judgement Training Manuals
  Judgement Training for Student Pilots
  Judgement Training for Instructor Pilots

Civil Aviation Authorities

UK – Aeronautical information circulars
Australia – Aviation safety digests
Bureau of Air Safety Investigation, Australia – BASI Journal

Association publications

Aircraft Owners and Pilots Association (AOPA) Safety Foundation (US)

Flight instructor safety reports

Aeronautical decision making
   Student and Private Pilot Manual
   Instrument Pilot Manual
   Instructor Guidance Manual
Key problems in general aviation

Flight Safety Foundation (US)– Pilot decision making workshop 1985
International Air Transport Association (IATA) – Airline guide to human factors

Medical Study Group, British Airline Pilots Association (BALPA) – Fit to Fly
European General Aviation Safety Foundation
   Instructor safety bulletins

Books

Aeronautical Decision Making for Instrument Pilots by R. Jensen and J. Adrion, Aviation Research Associates.
Human Factors in Flight by F. Hawkins, Gower Technical Press
Human Factors in Aviation by E. Wiener and D. Nagel, Academic Press Inc.
Basic Aviation Medicine by M. Bagshaw (Danair Services)
Aeromedicine for Aviators by K. Read, Pitman Publishing
IFR Refresher Publications PIC Services (US)
Aviation Safety Publications Belvoir Publications (US)
Aviation Medicine 2nd ed. Edited by Ernsting and King (Butterworths)
Aviation Medicine by Harding and Mills (British Medical Association)

Magazines

Factors influencing the time of safe unconsciousness (TSU) for commercial jet passengers following decompression, by James G. Gaume. *Aerospace Medicine*, April 1970. *Aerospace Information Report (AIR) No. 822 and 825B* (Physiology Section) SAE Committee A-10.
Pilot Error *Flying Magazine*

Other publications

Airmanship, Judgement and Aviation Safety by A. Ashman and R. Telfer, Universities of Queensland and of Newcastle, Australia.

Index

abdominal gas, 19
ab initio, 121
abscesses, gum, 20
absence of consistency, 95
acceleration, 40, 92
accident
  examples, 135, 138
  summaries, 94
accommodation, vision, 26
acute fatigue, 62
aerodrome traffic zone, 32
aeromedical considerations, 3
aeromedical facts, 4
aeromedical requirements, 4
aerosols, 74
AFISO, 32
age, 93
aircraft
  inspection, 125, 132
  manuals, 150
  operation, 96, 129
  performance, xii
  placards, 150
airmanship, 121
air safety, xi
air sickness, 50
airspace environment, 116
air traffic control, 32
alarm reaction, stress, 107
alcohol, 48, 50 *et seq*, 114
allergic rash, 58
altimeter, 147, 148
alveoli, 8
amphetamines, 59
anaesthetics, 60

analgesics, 59, 60
analysis of events, 130
anger, 68
angina, 66, 67
angular acceleration, 40
anthropometry, 147
anti-allergic drugs, 58
anti-authority, 129
antibiotics, 59
anticipation, 95
anti-histamines, 58
anti-hypertensives, 59
anxiety, xii, 48, 68, 110
apathy, 48
argon, 4
arousal, xiii, 4, 8, 62, 106
arrogance, 131
artificial horizon, 148
Ashman, Professor, 107, 112
asphyxia, 82
asthma, 58, 108
atheroma, 66, 67
atmosphere, 4, 8
atmospheric illusions, 34
atmospheric pressure, 10
attention getter, 150
attention getting stimuli, 99, 152
attention sources, 99 *et seq*
attention, specific item, 98
attitude development, 128
attitude indicator, 149
audio communications, 98
auditory nerve, 40
auditory ossicles, 39
authorised medical examiner, 4, 60

auto-kinesis, 34
automatic response, 6, 9, 97

backache, 52
bacterial infection, 54
balance mechanism, 39, 92
barbiturates, 59
barotrauma, 19
'behavioural' aspects
  anti authority, 129, 130
  change, 122
  complacency, 129, 132
  impulsiveness, 129, 130
  invulnerability, 129, 130
  machismo complex, 129, 131
  patterns, xi
  resignation, 129, 131
  reversion, 96
bends, 7, 20
binocular vision, 32
biological clock, 63
blackout, 21
bladder problems, 79
bleeding, 81, 84
blind spot, vision, 25
blood
  alcohol level, 56
  capillaries, 8
  donation, 61
  pressure, 59, 66, 108
  sugar, 50, 66
bloodstream, 11
blowby, 76
body
  cavities, 14
  height, 65
  temperature, 85
  weight, 10, 65
boredom, 61
Boyle's law, 5, 6, 19, 41
brain, 92
  connecting cells, 101
  damage, 101
  error correcting, 122
  error detecting, 122
  error making, 122
  function, 92, 101
  power, 101

stimulus, 92
breathing
  cycle, 14
  exercises, 114
broken limbs, 81, 83
bronchioles, 8
bronchus, 8
burns, 81, 86

cabin heating systems, 76
cabin pressurisation, 13 *et seq*
caffeine, 67
carbon dioxide, 4, 5, 8, 9
carbon monoxide, 26, 74, 79, 108
carbon monoxide detectors, 77
carburettor hot air system, 136
cardiovascular system, 66, 67, 79, 107
carelessness, 135, 136
cataracts, 65
causal factors, 123
central decision channel, 97
central nervous system, 55, 59, 101
certificate of airworthiness, 76
chain of events, 118, 123, 124
challenge and response system, 143
Charles's law, 5, 6
checklists, 63, 65, 153
chokes, 20
cholesterol, 67
chronic catarrh, 53
chronic fatigue, 62
chunking, 103
cinnarizine, 50
circadian low, 63
circadian rhythms, 62, 79
circulatory system, 8, 62
closure speeds, 27
cochlea, 39
cockpit
  environment, 98
  fenestration, 147
  management, 128, 142, 143
  placards, 150
  resource management, 144
  visibility, 147
cognition, xii
cognitive
  ability, 97

dissonance, 95
judgement, 122, 134, 135
perception, 96
collision course, 24 *et seq*
collision risk, 28
colour coded instruments, 150
colour vision, 37
coma, 85
combined instrument displays, 150
common drugs, 50
communication
  audio, 98
  channels, 94
competence
  comprehension based, 12
  knowledge based, 122
  rule based, 122
  skill based, 122
complacency, 129, 132, 138
complexity, airspace system, 129
complex rules, 118
compliance, 131
comprehension based competence,
  122
compressed gases, 74
compulsion, 135, 136, 138
concentration, 98
conceit, 131
concepts of
  arousal, 4, 8, 62, 106
  attention, 98
  central decision channel, 97
  compliance, 131
  conformity, 131
  memory, 101 *et seq*
  risky shift, 131
  sensation, 93
  stress, 105 *et seq*
cones, 23, 25, 33
confidence, 132
confirmation bias, 144
conformity, 131
conspicuity, 31
contact lens, 33
contentment, 132
continuous activity, 102
continuous flow, oxygen, 12, 16
cornea, 22

corrosive liquids, 14
cramps, 54
crew co-ordination, 143, 144, 145
cross checking, 144
cumulative stress, 108
cyclical change, 62

Dalton's law, 5, 6, 9
data evaluation, 122
deafness, 65
deceleration, 92
decision making, xii, 92, 96, 97, 119
decompression
  aircraft, 13 *et seq*
  diving, 80
  sickness, 7
deep breathing exercises, 114
deep sleep, 106
defective colour vision, 37
density, 5, 9
dental decay, 20
de-oxygenation, 17
depression, 48
depth perception, 30, 32, 58
design
  cockpit deficiencies, 146
  load factor, 105
desynchronosis, 63
deteriorating weather, 111
deterioration
  cognitive process, 117
  judgement, 117
  psychomotor ability, 117
  weather, 111, 117
diabetes, 65, 67
diaphragm, eyes, 22
diarrhoea, 52
diastolic pressure, 66
diet, 52, 66
diluter, oxygen, 16
discipline, 130
dissolved gas, 80
disorientation, 33, 41, 46, 56
disregard of regulations, 129
dissonance, 95
distracting
  influences, xii, 99
  situations, 116

ditching, 71
diverted attention, 94
domestic stressors, 108
dominant personality, 131
double check method, 104
drugs, 50
duty of care, 52

eardrum, 39 *et seq*, 52
earplugs, 43
educational programmes, xi
Edwards, Professor, 116
electrocardiogram, 66
emergency
    exits, 70
    pilot induced, 94
emotional
    anxiety, 68
    disturbance, 52, 96
    illness, 62
    stress, 52
    tension, 108
endolymph, 48
engine checks, 137
engine demand, 137
environment, 134
environmental stressors, 108
epilepsy, 47
equilibrium, senses, 33
ergonomics, 146, 147
erroneous
    actions, 93
    mental models, 33 *et seq*, 44, 45, 46
    messages, 91
ethyl alcohol, 55
euphoria, 56
European Civil Aviation Conference,
    144
Eustachian tube, 39 *et seq*, 52, 79
evaluation of data, 122
excess nitrogen, 80
exhaustion, 107
exhaust system, 76
expectancy, 95
experience, flight, 120
explosive decompression, 14
eye movements, 25

fail safe procedures, 149
false impressions, 91
fatigue, xiii, 61, 79, 96, 108
fear, 68
fire extinguishers, 73
first aid kits, 87
fitness, 3, 5
flammable liquids, 73
flashing lights, 47
flight
    crew licensing, 144
    instruments, 93
    lesson, 121
    phase, 109
    training philosophy, 128
flotation devices, 70
flow indicator, oxygen, 12 *et seq*
flying
    experience, 132
    skills, 97
focussing, eyes, 29
forcing functions, 64
fractured limbs, 83
FREDA, 103
frustration, 68, 110
fuel
    flow, 137
    flow gauge, 126
    selector, 96
    tank filter, 137
    tank vents, 125
function, memory, 103

gases, 4
gas transfer, 9
gastroenteritis, 52, 54, 79
gastro-intestinal tract, 19
general health, 3
geographic disorientation, 95
glaucoma, 65
go-around, 138
good judgement, 123
go or no-go decision, 140
gradual deterioration, 132
gregarious attitude, 114, 131
grey-out, 21
groundbourne stressors
    emotional, 115

physiological, 115
group
  behaviour, 131
  decisions, 131
guidance procedures, 143
gum, abscesses, 20

haemoglobin, 8, 74
halo effect, 37
hardware, SHEL model, 116
harness, safety, 69
HASELL, 103
hay fever, 53, 58
hazards, compulsion, 130
headaches, 106, 108
head injuries, 81, 85
hearing, 3, 43
heart
  beat, 107
  disease, 66, 110
  rhythm, 66
heroin, 58
Henry's law, 5, 6
high workload, 116
hormones, 65, 107
human
  attitudes, 128
  failures, 118
  frailties, 118
  information process, 91 *et seq*
  traits, 122
humidity, 5
hydrogen, 4
hypertension, 66, 67, 110
hyperventilation, 17, 48
hypoglycaemia, 21
hypoxia, 10, 11

IFR, 143
ignition system, 137
illusions
  atmospheric, 34
  autokinetic, 34
  featureless terrain, 36
  ground lighting, 34
  head movements, 44
  landing errors, 34
  manoeuvring, 45

rain effect, 37
runway slope, 34
runway width, 35
IMC, 93, 134
impaired judgement, 58
impulsiveness, 129, 130
inadequate fuel flow, 125
inattention, 51
incorrect assumptions, 144
incorrect operation systems, 116
ineffective communication, 143
inference formed belief, 137
influences
  employment, 136
  personal aspirations, 136
  social, 136
information
  processing, 50, 101
  sources, 98
  transfer problems, 116
injuries, 82
inner ear, 39, 93, 94
insomnia, 105
instrument flight, 46
insufficient recall, 116
insulin, 66
intercostal muscles, 8
interface – man/machine, 116, 130
intellectual skills, xii
International Civil Aviation
    Organisation, 65
interpersonal communications, 143
intestinal
  problems, 62
  tract, 14
intraocular pressure, 65
intuition, 97
invulnerability, 129, 130, 138
irritability, 106

jet lag, 63
job performance, 115
judgement
  brain, 92
  cognitive, 96, 97, 119 *et seq*
  complex type, 133
  concepts, 117
  exercising, 123

perceptual, 119 *et seq*
poor, 123 *et seq*
simple type, 133
training, 107, 123
judgement and decision making
aircraft factors, 134
environmental influence, 134
modular concept, 116
pilot stresses, 134
time factor, 135
juggling time and events, 112

kidney disease, 65
knowledge
implementation, 122
memory, 111
recall, 102
skill, 121
transfer, 104, 122
quality, 122
knowledge based
behaviour, 122
competence, 122
Kwells, 50

lack of
knowledge, 136
self control, 131
lacrimal gland, 22
language difficulties, 116
learning curve, 132
lens, eye, 22
life stressors, 108
limitations
central decision channel, 97
mental workload, 98
line orientated flight training, 144
liver, 62
liveware, 116
look-in time, 26
loss of control, aircraft, 124
loudness, hearing, 42
LSD, 58

machine failures, 118
machismo complex, 129, 131
maintaining accurate mental models,
132

malaise, 50
man/machine interface, 116, 130
marijuana, 58
master controller, brain, 92
medical
certificate, 52, 110
examination, 3, 4, 51
flight test, 32
prescriptions, 58
medication, 51, 79
membranes, 9
memory
function, 103, 105
information store, 97
limitations, 104
long term, 102
motor, 101
recall, 101
repetition, 101
retention, 101
short term, 101
structure, 101 *et seq*
working, 103
mental
accuracy, 132
alertness, 61
capability, 58
capacity, 110
depression, 58
disturbance, 59, 110
impairment, 11
model, 94
overload, 98
performance, 51
pressure, 110
response, 108
workload, 98
messages, muscle and joints, 93
metabolism, 56
midair collision, 29
middle ear, 39
migraine, headaches, 108
minor ailments, 5
misinterpretation, instruments, 116,
146, 147, 150
mis-judgement, 118, 146
misleading information, 91, 92
misperception, 95

mis-read check lists, 116
mis-selection, system controls, 146
mnemonics, 103
motion
  sensing system, 94
  sickness, 49, 57, 68
motor
  responses, 97
  skills, 121, 133
mucous membrane, 52, 53
multi-crew operations, 143
multiple tasks, 118
muscular co-ordination, 55
myopia, 25
myopic, 25, 29

nausea, 46
navigational errors, 95
near miss, 29
neon, 4
nerve
  endings, 33
  impulses, 23
nervous system, 48
new training concepts, 128
nitrogen, 4, 80
noise, 43, 108
non-automated decisions, 98
non-compression diving, 80
non pressurised aircraft, 80
NOTAMS, 126

obesity, 65, 67
observance of regulations, 129
omni bearing selector, 149
one degree under, 47, 109
operational environment, 118
operations, single pilot, 104
optic
  chiasma, 23
  nerve, 23
optimum, 106
  performance, 106, 113
  stress, 106
organic camera, eye, 22
orientation, 48
outer ear, 39
overbreathing, *See* hyperventilation

overcommitment, stress, 112
overlearning, 102
overload, aircraft, 105
overrun accidents, 138, 139, 140
overstress, 105
oxidation, alcohol, 56
oxidising materials, 74
oxygen
  atmosphere, 4
  diffusion, 8
  masks, 15
  partial pressure, 9 *et seq*
  passengers, 71
  regulator, 12 *et seq*
  systems, 12 *et seq*
ozone, 4

pancreas, 65
panic, 106
PAPI installation, 34
partial pressure oxygen, 9
peer pressure, 129, 142
penicillins, 59
perception
  aural, 97
  expectancy, 94
  physical, 94, 97
  visual, 94, 97
perceptual judgement, 119
performance
  deterioration, 107
  peak, 108
peripheral vision, 24, 30
personality, 123
personal pre-judgement, 145
photosynthesis, 5
physical
  action, 94
  activity, 51
  exercise, 64
  fitness, 52
  performance, 51
  response, 108
  senses, 91
  skill, 3
  stress, 134
photosensitive, lens, 26
physiological

altitude limits, 15
  factors, 51
  stress, 134
pilot
  discipline, 130
  distractions, 118
  induced emergency, 94
  judgement concepts, 116
  responsibility, 131, 136
  stress, 105
  training programmes, xiii, 144, 145
plastic lens implants, 65
poor judgement, 123
positive G, 20
posture, body, 64
power plant failure, 118
precognitive control, 122
pre-flight planning, 126
pre-occupation, 93, 143
presbyacusis, 43
presbyopia, 32
pressure demand, oxygen, 16
pressure point, 84
pressurisation, 17
pressurised cabin, 17, 80
procedure guide, 143
processing system, 92
proprioceptive senses, 33, 93
psychoactive drugs, 58
psychological
  behaviour, 91
  factors, 51
  pressures, 123
  stress, 62, 123, 134
pulse rate, 86

QNH, 93
qualified judgements, 143
quality
  cognitive perception, 122
  experience, 122
  judgement, 123
  knowledge, 122
  sensory perception, 122
  skill, 122

radar limitations, 31
radio communications, 31, 100

reactive stressors, 108, 115
reasoning, 97
re-breather bag, oxygen, 16
recall, 102, 116
receptors
  muscles, 92
  vision, 23
recovery position, 82
regulations, 135
relative movement, 28
resentment, 143
resignation, 129, 131
respiratory centre, brain, 17
rest cycle, eyes, 29
retina, 23
reversal phenomenon, oxygen, 17
risk
  aircraft, 123
  assessment, 134
  elements, 132
  environment, 123
  factors, 123
  management, 128
  pilot judgement, 123
  recognition, 133
  time available, 123
risky shift, 131
rods, eyes, 24, 33
rotating beacon, 47
rote actions, 130
RPM
  indicators, 150
  magneto check, 136
RTF messages, 98
rule based
  behaviour, 122
  competence, 122

saccade, 29
safety
  altitude, 127, 140
  appreciation, xiii
  harness/belt, 69
scanning, 24 *et seq*
scuba diving, 7
Sea Bands, 50
seat
  adjustment, 69

harness/belt, 14
sedatives, 58, 64
see and avoid, 26
selective attention, 99
self imposed obligations, 112
SELYE, 107
semi-circular canals, 39, 48 *et seq*
senses, 93
sensory
  illusions, 4
  information, 48, 92
  organs, 92
  perception, 103
  system, 92, 93, 94
serial tasks, 102
set, 95
severe shock, 81, 85
SHEL concept, 116
sickness, 48
simulator training, 144
single pilot operations, 104
sinuses, 19, 52 *et seq*, 79
situational awareness, 95, 120, 130,
  143, 146
skill based
  behaviour, 122
  competence, 122
skills
  acquisition, 121 *et seq*
  automatic behaviour, 143, 144
  conscious behaviour, 143
  errors of skill, 97, 116, 143
  nature of skill, 121, 122
sleep cycle, 52, 63
smoking, 69
social commitments, 135
sociological stress, 134
spatial disorientation
  management, 33, 44
  recognition, 33 *et seq*, 44 *et seq*
splints, 83
spring fever, 132
stall
  aircraft, 123
  warner, 98, 99
standard atmosphere, 9
status differential, 143
stick shakers, 65

stimulants, 64
stimulus, 98
stomach upsets, 54, 62, 108
stress
  alarm stage, 107
  arousal, 106
  body, 105
  cumulative, 108
  effects, 111
  emotional, 108
  environmental, 108
  domestic, 108
  identification, 113
  insidious, 111
  limit, 109
  management, 128
  optimum, 106
  overcommitment, 112
  overload, 111
  pilot, 105
  reduction, 113
  sociological, 134
  time induced, 111
  warning signs, 112, 113
stressors, 107, 134
strobe lights, 47
stroboscopic, 47
stroke, 66
supplementary oxygen, 9, 12 *et seq*
Stugeron, 50
systems failure, 118
systolic pressure, 66

take-off, approach and landing, 138
tangling words, 93
task
  requirements, 138
  saturation, 116
team management, 143
Telfer, Professor, 107, 112
temperament, 123
temperature, 5
tetracyclines, 59
thinking cells, brain, 55
thinktank, 92
time
  constraints, 122
  controlling influence, 135

induced stress, 111
  keeping, 114
  of useful consciousness, 15
  zones, 63
tiredness, 61
tobacco smoking, 11
tolerance G, 21
tone, hearing, 43
touch and go landings, 138
toxic
  agents, 73
  fumes, 73
  goods, 73
trachea, 8, 14
traditional flight training, 128
training
  experience, 132
  programmes, 102, 144
transponder, 144

unconsciousness, 56
underconfidence, 131
unnecessary risks, 130
unpopular decisions, 131
unproven fuel flow, 137
unreasonable requests, 131
unsafe requests, 131
unserviceable airspeed indicator, 136
upper torso
  movement, 147
  restraint, 79
urine analysis, 65
use of checklists, 145

vascular organ, 56
VASI installation, 34
verbal communication, 100
vertigo, 46
vestibular
  organs, 44
  system, 50, 91
VFR, 127
vibration, 108

viral infection, 54
visibility, cockpit, 147
vision
  central, 24
  limitations, 24 *et seq*
  peripheral, 24
visual
  acuity, 24
  checking, 94
  cortex, 23
  field, 26
  reference, 47
  search techniques, 26
visual cues, 33
vital information, 100
vivid occurrences, 102
VMC, 107, 134, 143
vomiting, 47, 49
VOR, 149

warning
  flags, 65
  horns, 65
  information, 150
  lights, 65
warning signs, stress, 112, 113, 114
weariness, 62
weather
  deterioration, 111, 141
  related risks, 140
wellbeing, 114
windshear, 107
wishful thinking, 115
workload
  overcommitment, 112
  regulations, 129
  self-imposed, 146
  spreading, 142
  system failures, 118
workspace constraints, 146
worry, 110, 115

Yerkes-Dodson curve, 106